A Streetcar Named Desire

AF190499

Tennessee Williams

Notes and activities: Annie Fox
Series consultant: Peter Buckroyd

Oxford
Literature
Companions

OXFORD
UNIVERSITY PRESS

Contents

Introduction

What are Oxford Literature Companions?

Oxford Literature Companions is a series designed to provide you with comprehensive support for popular set texts. You can use the Companion alongside your play, using relevant sections during your studies or using the book as a whole for revision.

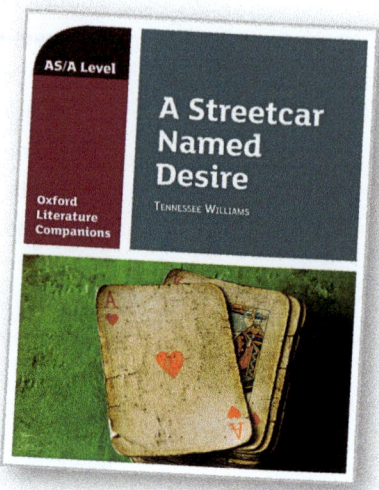

Each Companion includes detailed guidance and practical activities on:

- **Plot and Structure**
- **Context**
- **Genre**
- **Characterization and Roles**
- **Language**
- **Themes**
- **Performance**
- **Critical Views**
- **Skills and Practice**

How does this book help with exam preparation?

As well as providing guidance on key areas of the play, throughout this book you will also find 'Upgrade' features. These are tips to help with your exam preparation and performance.

In addition, in the extensive **Skills and Practice** chapter, the 'Exam skills' section provides detailed guidance on areas such as how to prepare for the exam, understanding the question, planning your response and hints for what to do (or not do) in the exam.

In the **Skills and Practice** chapter there is also a bank of **Sample questions** and **Sample answers**. The **Sample answers** are marked and include annotations and a summative comment.

How does this book help with terminology?

Throughout the book, key terms are **highlighted** in the text and explained on the same page. There is also a detailed **Glossary** at the end of the book that explains, in the context of the play, all the relevant literary terms highlighted in this book.

Which edition of the play has this book used?

Quotations and character names have been taken from the Penguin Modern Classics edition of *A Streetcar Named Desire* (ISBN 978-0-141-19027-3).

How does this book work?

Each book in the Oxford Literature Companions series follows the same approach and includes the following features:

- **Key quotations** from the play
- **Key terms** explained on the page and linked to a complete glossary at the end of the book
- **Activity boxes** to help improve your understanding of the text
- **Upgrade** tips to help prepare you for your assessment

Activity boxes to help improve your understanding of the play

Key terms explained on the page and at the end of the book

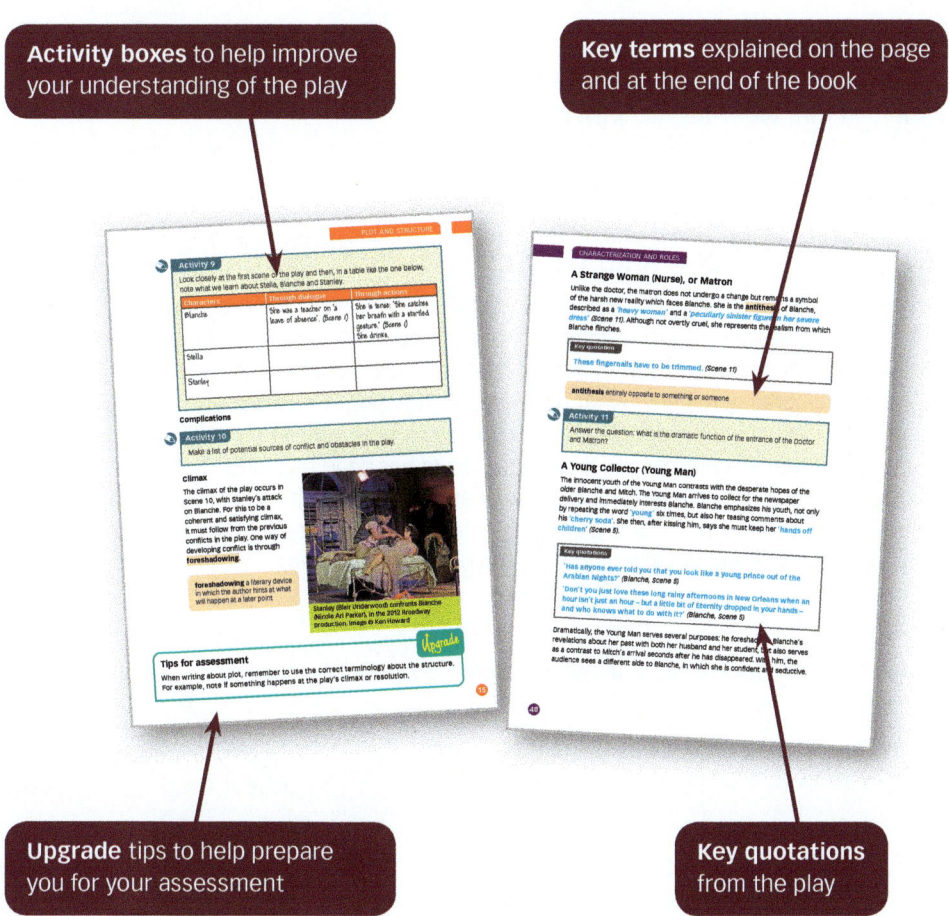

Upgrade tips to help prepare you for your assessment

Key quotations from the play

Plot and Structure

Plot

A Streetcar Named Desire follows Blanche DuBois, the play's **protagonist**, as she fights for a future in New Orleans, while clinging to the ghosts of her past.

Scene 1

Blanche, a former English teacher, arrives at the New Orleans apartment of her sister Stella and her Polish-American husband Stanley Kowalski. Blanche is nervous and highly strung, clearly surprised by the very basic conditions in which Stella is living. Blanche confesses to Stella that Belle Reve, their family's home, has been lost due to the profligate ways of their family and the demands of their many creditors. Blanche reprimands Stella: *'I let the place go? Where were you? In bed with your – Polak!'* Stanley and Blanche meet. When Stanley asks if Blanche has been married, she says 'the boy died' and that she feels sick.

> **Key quotation**
>
> **You'll get along fine together, if you'll just try not to – well – compare him with men that we went out with at home.** *(Stella)*

Scene 2

The next evening: Stella tells Stanley that the Belle Reve estate has been lost. Stanley is suspicious, claiming **'we have the Napoleonic code according to which what belongs to the wife belongs to the husband and vice versa'**. He goes through Blanche's belongings, looking for evidence of her having used the money from the estate. When Blanche returns from her bath, the two have a charged conversation, with Stanley demanding to know what happened to the money and Blanche responding by flirting and evading: **'I was fishing for a compliment, Stanley.'** Finally, angered that Stanley has touched letters from her dead husband, Blanche hands Stanley a box of documents about the estate. Stanley explains that he has to look after their interests as Stella is expecting a baby. The men begin to arrive for Stanley's poker party, and Blanche and Stella go out for the evening.

> **Key quotations**
>
> **If I didn't know that you was my wife's sister I'd get ideas about you!** *(Stanley)*
>
> **Poems a dead boy wrote. I hurt him the way that you would like to hurt me, but you can't!** *(Blanche)*

Activity 1

In Scene 2, we see the first confrontation between Blanche and Stanley. Write a paragraph explaining which character you have more sympathy for at the end of this scene and why. Choose at least four quotations to support your point of view.

Scene 3

Hours later: Stanley is angry because he is losing at the poker game. His friend and workmate Mitch says he needs to look after his ill mother. Stella and Blanche return from their night out. Stella asks Stanley to bring the game to a close and Stanley gives her a *'whack'* on her thigh. Blanche meets Mitch and he gives her a cigarette. He tells her about the girl, now dead, who gave him the cigarette case. Blanche turns on the radio and begins dancing, to

The Night Café by Vincent Van Gogh

Mitch's delight. Stanley throws the radio out of the window and then hits Stella. Stella goes to a neighbour's apartment. The men attempt to sober up Stanley. Stanley shouts for Stella. She eventually returns and they embrace. Mitch and Blanche sit on the steps outside the apartment and she thanks him for being kind.

Activity 2

This scene is subtitled 'The Poker Night', which was also one of the titles Williams considered for the whole play, suggesting it is a very important scene. In the **stage directions** for Scene 3, Williams compares the setting to the painting by Van Gogh shown on this page.

a) Read through the stage directions and examine the painting.

b) Then write at least five bullet points explaining what Williams wanted to convey about this scene through these stage directions.

protagonist the central character, who must overcome obstacles in an attempt to achieve a goal

stage directions written instructions conveying the appearance and actions of the play

Scene 4

The next morning: Blanche urges Stella to leave Stanley. Despite Stella saying she doesn't wish to leave, Blanche begins making plans involving an old college beau of hers, Shep Huntleigh, to whom she wants to send a telegram. Stella says she loves Stanley and tries to calm Blanche down, but Blanche says Stanley is 'an animal'. Unknown to her, Stanley overhears her complaints about him. When he enters, he pretends he hasn't heard. Stella and he embrace, while he grins at Blanche.

Scene 5

Upstairs neighbours Steve and Eunice have a noisy fight, while Blanche writes a letter to Shep. Stanley tells Blanche about a man called Shaw who knows people in Laurel, Blanche's hometown. After Stanley leaves, Blanche asks Stella what she has heard about her. Blanche has a drink and says she is nervous about her upcoming date with Mitch. She talks about wanting Mitch because a relationship with him would finally allow her to 'rest'. After Stella leaves, a Young Man appears to collect the payment for the newspaper delivery. Blanche flirts with him and kisses him. Just after he leaves, Mitch appears, carrying a bouquet of roses.

> **Key quotation**
>
> I want to *rest*! I want to breathe quietly again! Yes – I *want* Mitch... *very badly*!
> (Blanche)

Scene 6

Later that same night: Blanche and Mitch return to the Kowalski apartment. They drink and flirt awkwardly. She asks Mitch if Stanley has talked to him about her. She describes how difficult she finds living in the Kowalski apartment. Mitch asks her age, as his mother would like to know, and Blanche evades answering. She explains that she knows what it is like to be lonely and describes the death of her husband Allan Grey, who killed himself after she had confronted him on the dance floor: 'I'd suddenly said – "I know! I know! You disgust me..."'. Mitch comforts her and takes her into his arms.

> **Key quotation**
>
> He was in the quicksands and clutching at me – but I wasn't holding him out, I was slipping in with him!
> (Blanche)

offstage character a character not seen on stage

Scene 7

While Stella is preparing a small birthday supper for Blanche, Stanley tells Stella that he has learned the truth about Blanche. He has been told she was thrown out of the Flamingo Hotel in Laurel and lost her teaching job because of her behaviour. Stella says she doesn't believe these stories, although Blanche had always been **'flighty'** due in part to her disastrous marriage to a young man who was a **'degenerate'**. Stanley says that Mitch is **'wised up'** to Blanche and won't be coming to the birthday party. Stanley has bought a bus ticket for Blanche to leave on Tuesday.

> **Key quotation**
>
> **Yep, it was practickly a town ordinance passed against her!**
> *(Stanley)*

Scene 8

Forty-five minutes later: Stanley, Stella and Blanche are finishing the birthday dinner, with an empty seat left for Mitch. Blanche tells a joke, which falls flat. Stella says that Stanley is making a **'pig'** of himself. Stanley hurls the dishes onto the floor. Later Blanche calls Stanley a **'healthy Polack'**, which further infuriates him. He presents Blanche with her birthday gift, a single one-way ticket back to Laurel. Blanche runs from the room. Stella goes into labour and Stanley takes her to the hospital.

> **Key quotation**
>
> **'Pig – Polack – disgusting – vulgar – greasy!' – them kind of words have been on your tongue and your sister's too much around here!**
> *(Stanley)*

Scene 9

Later that evening: Blanche is wearing a satin robe and drinking, when Mitch arrives. Blanche keeps hearing the Varsouviana polka and says **'That – music again…'**, which makes Mitch believe she is drunk. He tells her to lay off Stanley's liquor. He tears off the paper lantern on the light and insists on looking at her. He accuses her of lying to him. The Mexican flower vendor can be heard outside. Mitch embraces Blanche but says he no longer wants to marry her because she isn't **'clean enough to bring in the house with my mother'**. Blanche screams **'Fire!'** to escape him and Mitch leaves.

Mitch (Karl Malden) scrutinizes Blanche (Vivien Leigh) under the light in the 1951 film

---

Key quotation

I don't mind you being older than what I thought. But all the rest of it – God! That pitch about your ideals being so old-fashioned and all the malarkey that you've dished out all summer. Oh, I knew you weren't sixteen any more. But I was a fool enough to believe you was straight. *(Mitch)*

Activity 4

We see a very different Mitch in this scene.

a) Compare his behaviour in Scenes 6 and 9 in a table like the one below.

	Scene 6	Scene 9
Mitch's appearance		
Mitch's dialogue		
Mitch's actions		

b) Now write a paragraph explaining how and why Mitch's behaviour towards Blanche has changed. You might begin: 'It is clear that Mitch's feelings towards Blanche have changed between Scene 6 and Scene 9. In Scene 6, Williams shows Mitch to be….'

Scene 10

A few hours later: Blanche has been drinking, dressing up and packing her trunk. She puts on a tiara and begins addressing imaginary admirers. Stanley enters and says the baby hasn't been born yet, so he has returned to get some rest. Blanche claims she has had an invitation from an old admirer. At first, Stanley plays along with her but then he accuses her of **'lies and conceit and tricks!'** Blanche attempts to make contact with Shep Huntleigh. Stanley enters and hangs up the telephone. As he menacingly approaches her, Blanche breaks a bottle but Stanley overcomes her.

Activity 5

It is a matter of interpretation why Stanley attacks Blanche in this scene.

a) What reasons can you think of for his attack?

b) Look at the following bullet points and decide which interpretation is closest to yours.

- From the moment Stanley enters the scene he plans to attack Blanche.
- Blanche has been encouraging Stanley all along.
- The attack is a spur of the moment decision.
- This is the only way Stanley knows to bring Blanche down.

c) Read through the scene from **'I've been on to you from the start!'** to **'We've had this date with each other from the beginning!'**, trying different interpretations and deciding which one works best.

Scene 11

A few weeks later: the original poker players Pablo, Steve, Mitch and Stanley are playing cards again while Eunice and Stella speak about **'arrangements for her [Blanche] to rest in the country'**. Blanche emerges from the bathroom and worries about what she is going to wear. There is tension between the two sides of the apartment as Mitch is aware of Blanche's presence and Blanche is fearful of Stanley's. A doctor and matron arrive. When Blanche realizes it isn't Shep Huntleigh she becomes fearful. The matron tries to subdue her and Stanley tears down the paper lantern and hands it to her. Mitch accuses Stanley of causing all this trouble with his **'God damn interfering'**. The doctor addresses her kindly. Blanche's *'terror subsides a little'* and she takes his arm and leaves, saying, **'I have always depended on the kindness of strangers'**. Stella cries. Stanley kneels beside her to comfort her. The remaining men continue to play poker.

> **Key quotations**
>
> **I couldn't believe her story and go on living with Stanley.** (*Stella*)
>
> **This game is seven-card stud.** (*Steve*)

11

Structure

Traditionally, plays are divided into acts. Shakespeare's plays are separated into five acts, Ibsen's *A Doll's House* is in three acts and Chekhov's *The Cherry Orchard*, considered to be an influence on Williams, has four acts. However *A Streetcar Named Desire* is not divided into more traditional acts, but instead consists of eleven **episodic** scenes. In some productions the play is given two intervals (the original put these after Scenes 4 and 6), while some have a single interval and others perform the play straight through with no breaks.

Activity 6

Use a table like the one below to note the key events of each scene. Complete a row for every scene from 1 to 11.

	Key actions	Key quotations
Scene 1	Blanche arrives at Stella and Stanley's apartment.	'They told me to take a streetcar named Desire, and then transfer to one called Cemeteries and ride six blocks and get off at – Elysian Fields!'
Scene 2		
Scene 3		

Climax and anti-climax

Unlike the more typical three-act structure where each act reaches a **climax**, each of the eleven scenes in this play reaches a climax and then ends with an **anti-climactic**, often more reflective, moment.

> **anti-climactic** a descent or retreat from the intensity of the climax
>
> **climax** the most intense moment
>
> **episodic** a series of loosely connected episodes or scenes which may depict a period of time

For example, Scene 3 might be charted as follows:

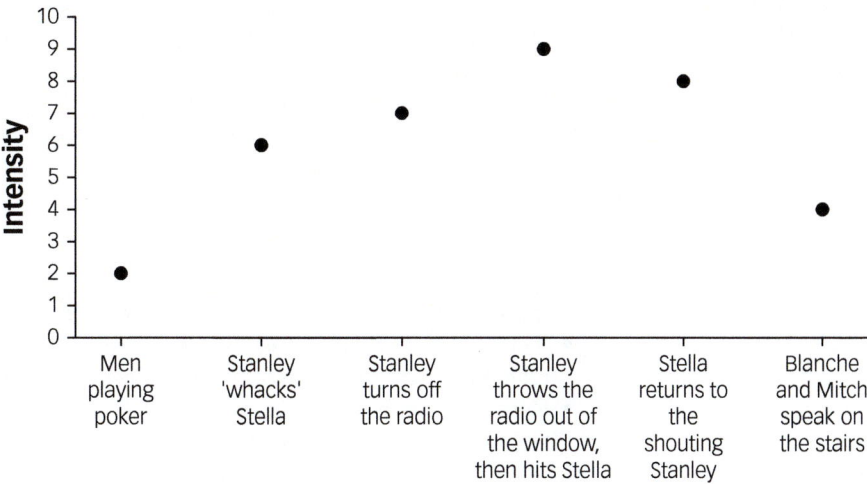

Key incidents

Activity 7

Choose another scene from the play and chart the key events and levels of intensity in the same way on a graph. Then identify the climax and anti-climax.

Handling of time and the unities

The ancient Greek writer Aristotle wrote about the nature of tragedy. In his *Poetics* he advocated the 'three unities', which were:

- unity of action (one main plot with few diversions or subplots)
- unity of time (the action should take place over no more than 24 hours)
- unity of place (the action should take place in a single location representing a single place).

Williams concentrates on Blanche's journey in the play and she is rarely offstage. The Kowalski flat and its immediate surroundings form the single location. However, Williams does not adhere to the unities in his handling of time. Instead of the recommended 24 hours, the play takes place over roughly six months. The first scene is set in the **'first dark of an evening early in May'** and this is reinforced by Blanche saying she has left her school **'before the spring term ended'**. Some scenes follow minutes or hours upon the previous one, while between others there are gaps of weeks or months. This length of time is needed for several practical reasons: Stella's pregnancy is barely showing in the first scene, yet she goes into labour in Scene 8 and has brought the baby home by Scene 11; Mitch needs time to meet, court and consider marrying Blanche; Stanley has to put into motion his plan to discover Blanche's past and to hear back from his salesman friend the rumours from Laurel.

Activity 8

Use a table like the one below to note key moments when time, seasons or weather are mentioned to increase the atmosphere of the scenes.

Month/Season	Scenes/Actions/Notes	Key quotations
May		
August	Heat is emphasized. • 'fanning herself with a palm leaf' (Scene 5) • Mitch is ashamed of how he perspires.	'Don't you just love these long rainy afternoons in New Orleans when an hour isn't just an hour – but a little bit of Eternity dropped in your hands – and who knows what to do with it?' (Blanche, Scene 5)
September (15 September, Blanche's birthday)		
October ('some weeks' after the previous scene)		

Dramatic structural features

Although episodically written and not adhering to the tight time constraints of classic tragedy, Williams's play nevertheless clearly adheres to many conventional demands of drama, including:

- **Exposition:** establishing the setting, characters and their backgrounds. Possible sources of conflict are identified.
- **Complications:** conflicts occur and problems are presented.
- **Climax:** the development of the conflict reaches its high point.
- **Falling action:** the consequences of the climax are felt.
- **Resolution:** the conflict is resolved, either through catastrophe or triumph.

Exposition

Unlike novelists, who can simply have narrators discussing the backgrounds of their characters, dramatists must rely on the dialogue and characters' actions to reveal their pasts.

Activity 9

Look closely at the first scene of the play and then, in a table like the one below, note what we learn about Stella, Blanche and Stanley.

Characters	Through dialogue	Through actions
Blanche	She was a teacher on 'a leave of absence'. (Scene 1)	She is tense: 'She catches her breath with a startled gesture.' (Scene 1) She drinks.
Stella		
Stanley		

Complications

 Activity 10

Make a list of potential sources of conflict and obstacles in the play.

Climax

The climax of the play occurs in Scene 10, with Stanley's attack on Blanche. For this to be a coherent and satisfying climax, it must follow from the previous conflicts in the play. One way of developing conflict is through **foreshadowing**.

> **foreshadowing** a literary device in which the author hints at what will happen at a later point

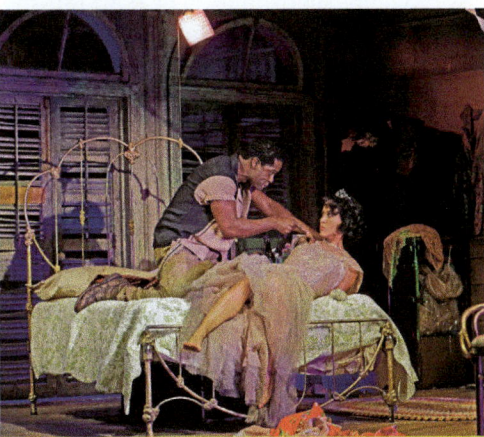

Stanley (Blair Underwood) confronts Blanche (Nicole Ari Parker) in the 2012 Broadway production. Image © Ken Howard

Tips for assessment

When writing about plot, remember to use the correct terminology about the structure. For example, note if something happens at the play's climax or resolution.

Activity 11

a) Look at the quotations below and consider how they may foreshadow the climactic assault of Stanley upon Blanche.

- **Stanley:** **Do you mind if I make myself comfortable?** [*He starts to remove his shirt.*]

  Blanche: **Please, please do.**
  (Scene 1)

- **Excuse me while I slip on my pretty new dress!!** *(Blanche, Scene 2)*

- **I'm going to ask a favour of you in a moment.** *(Blanche, Scene 2)*

- **Would you think it possible that I was once considered to be – attractive?** *(Blanche, Scene 2)*

- **If I didn't know that you was my wife's sister I'd get ideas about you!** *(Stanley, Scene 2)*

- *He stops short at sight of Blanche in the chair. She returns his look without flinching.* *(Scene 3)*

- *There is the sound of a blow. Stella cries out. Blanche screams and runs into the kitchen.* *(Scene 3)*

- **What such a man has to offer is animal force and he gave a wonderful exhibition of that! But the only way to live with such a man is to – go to bed with him! And that's your job – not mine!** *(Blanche, Scene 4)*

- **Come to think of it – maybe you wouldn't be bad to – interfere with...** *(Stanley, Scene 10)*

b) At the end of Scene 10, Stanley says, **'We've had this date with each other from the beginning!'** Write a paragraph explaining to what extent you agree with this statement.

Falling action

After the climactic action of Scene 10, Scene 11 opens in a more minor key with the Kowalski household apparently restored to some kind of normality. It lacks the tension of the climax and leads to the play's ending. The early sections of Scene 11 contain the play's **falling action**, where the effects of Stanley's rape of Blanche are revealed. His actions have affected Blanche's mental state, her relationship with her sister, and her future, while he has returned to being **'king'** of his house.

Resolution

The resolution or **denouement** is the end of the play, which brings together the loose ends. The ending of *A Streetcar Named Desire* is a controversial one as some viewers feel that Stanley goes unpunished for his actions. When the play was filmed, this was one of the main points that studio censors insisted was changed. However, some people note that Stella and Mitch both feel guilt and anguish at Blanche's treatment. The **'kindness'** of the doctor also gives some hope that Blanche will be well treated in the asylum, though it is hard to view her exit as anything more than a defeat.

> **denouement** the final part of a play or film, when the various plot strands are concluded
>
> **falling action** the section of the plot between the climax and the resolution, which often focuses on the direct consequences of the climax

Activity 12

Read the quotations below and then write a paragraph explaining how effective you find the ending of the play, including a discussion of these key moments.

- **I don't know if I did the right thing.** *(Stella, Scene 11)*

- **Don't ever believe it. Life has got to go on. No matter what happens, you've got to keep on going.** *(Eunice, Scene 11)*

- *Mitch collapses at the table, sobbing. (Scene 11)*

- [*a bit uncertainly*]: **Stella?** *(Stanley, Scene 11)*

- **This game is seven-card stud.** *(Steve, Scene 11)*

Writing about plot and structure

Use the checklist below to evaluate your own writing about plot and structure.

- Remember to analyse the plot; don't just retell it.

- Use the correct terminology when writing about the play, such as 'stage directions', 'scenes', 'exposition' and 'characterization'.

- Consider when events occur and the time that passes between scenes.

- Discuss how the scenes are shaped by conflict, obstacles, increases in tension and resolutions.

- Identify the climax of the scenes and the play.

- Consider how techniques such as foreshadowing influence your understanding of the play.

- Reflect on the demands of drama and forms of it, like tragedy, and to what extent this play meets those demands.

Biography of Tennessee Williams

- Thomas Lanier Williams (later to become Tennessee Williams) was born in Columbus, Mississippi on 26 March 1911.

- His father, Cornelius, who worked as a salesman, and his mother Edwina, the 'southern belle' daughter of a vicar, had a strained, unhappy marriage.

- The family lived for a while with their maternal grandparents in a rectory and later moved to St Louis, Missouri.

- As a child, Williams contracted diphtheria and was an invalid for two years. During this time he read and played imaginative games.

- Williams attended the University of Missouri where he discovered his love of writing and the theatre.

- His sister Rose, of whom Williams was very fond, developed severe mental health problems resulting in a move to a sanatorium.

Tennessee Williams on the set of the original 1947 Broadway production

- Williams moved to New Orleans in 1938 where he began writing under the name Tennessee Williams. He won an award for his one-act plays, which led to his gaining the services of Audrey Wood, a powerful and influential agent.

- His first major play, *The Glass Menagerie*, inspired by his sister and mother's relationship, opened in 1944 and won many awards.

- In 1945, Williams began a two-year relationship with Pancho Rodriguez y Gonzalez, who was considered by many to be an inspiration for Stanley in *A Streetcar Named Desire*.

- *A Streetcar Named Desire* opened in New York on 3 December 1947 to great acclaim and won many prizes, including the Pulitzer Prize.

- A number of other important plays by Williams followed, including *The Rose Tattoo* (1950), *Cat on a Hot Tin Roof* (1955) and *Sweet Bird of Youth* (1956).

- The film of *A Streetcar Named Desire* was released in 1951.

- After the death of his long-term lover and personal secretary Frank Merlo in 1963, Williams succumbed to depression, alcoholism and drug dependency.

- Williams's plays continued to be frequently revived and performed around the world. He also continued to write, including *Vieux Carre* (1977).

- Williams died on 25 February 1983.

Biographical influences on *A Streetcar Named Desire*

In his writing, Williams used the colourful characters from his extended family whom he had studied from birth. The novelist and essayist Gore Vidal referred to Williams's family as forming a 'basic repertory company' from which he could draw inspiration.

Williams's relationship with his boyfriend Pancho, who had a passionate and violent nature, coloured his portrayal of Stanley. Once, in anger, Pancho threw Williams's typewriter out of the window, which is reminiscent of Stanley's disposal of the radio in a similar fashion in Scene 3. Blanche has aspects of Williams's mother (who behaved like a pampered southern belle), his sister (her mental instability) and Williams himself. Williams shared Blanche's tendency to drink, to fleeting intimacies and a sensitive, fragile mental state.

However, it is important not to take the connections between Williams's life and the characters of the play too literally. Williams carefully crafted his plays, often adjusting them in reaction to the advice of others, including creative collaborators like the director Elia Kazan. The play was developed through a series of drafts and rewrites. For example, the character of Stanley in earlier drafts was Italian and then Irish before Williams settled on Polish – very different from Pancho's Mexican background.

Activity 1

Read the above biographical comments about Williams and highlight any points you think may have a bearing on your understanding of *A Streetcar Named Desire*.

Upgrade

Tips for assessment

Facts about the playwright's life should only be included in your writing if they are directly relevant to the text of the play or if you are being asked to discuss the playwright's intentions in writing *A Streetcar Named Desire*.

Second World War

The Second World War (1939–1945) was a global war in which the American military fought as part of the Allied forces in Europe and beyond. *A Streetcar Named Desire* premiered just two years after the end of the war, when America was adjusting to changes in the social fabric of the country caused by the war. During the war, while the men were away, many women were encouraged to work in factories and to take charge of their households. Meanwhile, some men serving in the army gained skills and opportunities which would have previously been denied them. Many socialized with a wider range of people than those available in the neighbourhoods in which they grew up.

In *A Streetcar Named Desire*, the audience learns that Stanley worked as an army engineer where he became friends with Mitch. When Stella met Stanley he was in uniform, which Blanche felt was part of his attraction for Stella.

At the end of the war there was, for some, an uneasy transition as men returned to their civilian life to reclaim their jobs and positions within their homes. There was the possibility of greater fluidity between social classes, which sometimes caused conflict with those who were clinging onto an older social order.

Key quotation

Stella: A Master Sergeant in the Engineers' Corps. Those are decorations!

Blanche: He had those on when you met him?
(Scene 1)

Williams does not present Stanley simply as a decorated soldier who wants to return to a peaceful, ordered life. Although he is patriotic, declaring himself to be **'one hundred per cent American, born and raised in the greatest country on earth'** *(Scene 8)*, some critics, such as Camille Paglia, see him as a **harbinger** of the counter-culture that grew after the end of the war:

In its taboo-breaking style, *Streetcar* belonged to an oppositional strain in American culture that emerged following World War II. The near-universal patriotism of the war years, galvanized to defeat German and Japanese **imperialism**, continued in mainstream American society and media for nearly two decades. But it was countered by an underground variously represented by **abstract expressionism**, bebop, and the Beats, as well as **existentialism** imported from Paris. There was a touch of the cynical hipster in Brando's impudent delivery of Stanley's brusque, satirically deadpan lines.

(Camille Paglia, 'Tennessee Williams', *A New Literary History*)

Activity 2

Look at the quotations below and explain how each relates to the Second World War.

- **Stella: But of course there were things to adjust myself to later on.**

  Blanche: Such as his civilian background! *(Scene 1)*

- **Mitch is a buddy of mine. We were in the same outfit together – Two-forty-first Engineers. We work in the same plant and now on the same bowling team. You think I could face him if –** *(Stanley, Scene 7)*

- **Yes, did you know there was an army camp near Laurel and your sister's was one of the places called 'Out-of-Bounds'?** *(Stanley, Scene 7)*

Gender roles

A typical US housewife in the 1940s was responsible for all domestic duties

The war years saw an expansion in work opportunities for women, with some women serving in the armed forces and working in factories. Eleanor Roosevelt, the president's wife, served as the nation's First Lady from 1933 to 1945, and was a positive role model. In 1945 she became the US Delegate to the United Nations.

Although the percentage of women working greatly increased during the 1940s, the majority worked in traditional 'female occupations', such as clerical jobs, teaching and catering. Unusual opportunities, like the all-female professional baseball league, were temporary **anomalies** that disappeared a few years after the end of the war. There was a fear that women in attractive 'male' jobs would be reluctant to leave them when the soldiers returned from the war to reclaim their former positions. After the war, women were actively encouraged to return to the role of 'homemaker'.

abstract expressionism a post-Second World War art movement based on non-representational, apparently spontaneous work

anomalies unusual or odd cases

existentialism a philosophy which focuses on the will of the individual and is associated with a sense of alienation or disorientation in an absurd world

harbinger something or someone who signals or forecasts something

imperialism using force to extend a country's powers and borders

In the Kowalski household it is clear that Stanley expects to be the **'king'** with Stella arranging her life around his needs: his bowling, his poker playing, his meals and his bed. One of the sources of conflict is Blanche's disruption of his ordered home and her influence on Stella.

> **Key quotations**
>
> **How about my supper, huh? I'm not going to no Galatoires' for supper!** *(Stanley, Scene 2)*
>
> **Since when do you give me orders?** *(Stanley, Scene 2)*

Blanche's role can be viewed as **transgressive**. She defies expectations in many ways. After her marriage ends in tragedy, she takes a job teaching, which would have been socially acceptable. However she then breaks the boundaries of her professional responsibility by having an affair with a 17-year-old student. She flees her hometown after a succession of short-lived intimacies. In her interactions with Mitch she mimics the conventional courting rituals of flirtations and prim physical contact. By contrast, she is clearly the predator in her scene with the Young Man. Her actions confirm her sexually rebellious behaviour and would have been shocking to 1940s audiences. Although a rule-breaker, Blanche is not portrayed by Williams as a feminist: aside from a fleeting mention of setting up a shop with Stella, the only salvation she dreams of is either to be supported by a rich former beau or to settle for a safe, but improbable, married life with Mitch. However, some audience members may question how the restrictions and expectations of her society led to her mental instability and to Stella's betrayal of her.

Allan Grey, Blanche's dead husband, is another figure who challenges the expectations of the 1940s audience. Although not seen on stage, Williams clearly suggests that Blanche interrupts him with another man. In the 1940s homosexuality was rarely overtly mentioned in mainstream media or entertainment and was thought of as something to be condemned or even 'cured'. Homosexuality was considered to be a mental illness by many and homosexuals could be banned from certain jobs, like those in the military. In 1950, a Senate Report entitled 'Employment of Homosexuals and Other Sex Perverts in Government', concluded that the hiring of homosexuals was a security risk. Although Williams's writing is bold for his time, it is not explicit and uses a coded language which more sophisticated audiences would understand.

> **transgressive** breaking boundaries, rules, social orders or moral codes

> **Activity 3**
>
> Read Blanche's speech in Scene 6, which begins **'He was a boy, just a boy...'.**
> Highlight any words or phrases which provide insight into Grey's marriage to Blanche and the portrayal of gender roles in the play.

Social class and ethnic identity

Key quotation

Stanley: The Kowalskis and the DuBois have different notions.

Stella [*angrily*]: Indeed they have, thank heavens!'
(Scene 2)

One source of conflict in the play is the struggle between Blanche and Stanley as representatives of two contrasting and warring social classes. Blanche is a representative of the dying aristocracy, with its history of land-owning, education, etiquette and formal social gatherings. Stanley, on the other hand, is the son of Polish immigrants, proudly American and poorly educated. He seeks not only to advance himself, but is also determined to bring Blanche down, just as he 'pulled' Stella 'down off them columns' *(Scene 8)*. Williams establishes this conflict in the first scene, in which Stanley takes off his shirt moments after meeting Blanche, proclaiming, 'Be comfortable is my motto' *(Scene 1)*. He makes clear that the household is run according to his rules and others must adjust to them.

The contrast in their education is clear. While Blanche frequently speaks in a lyrical, heightened way and references favourite authors like Edgar Alan Poe or Elizabeth Barrett Browning, Stanley says, 'I never was a very good English student' *(Scene 1)*. When he does try to assert his intelligence by citing the 'Napoleonic code' he sounds clumsy and unconvincing. However, he is cunning, ultimately outwitting and overpowering Blanche. Blanche realizes his potential power, saying, 'But maybe he's what we need to mix with our blood now that we've lost Belle Reve and have to go on without Belle Reve to protect us' *(Scene 2)*.

Stanley aspires to the **American Dream**, believing that by hard work and determination he will achieve a higher standard of living than that of his parents, unlike Blanche who has fallen from a higher status. He is also influenced by politicians like Huey Long, whom he quotes in the play. Huey Long was a controversial 1930s Louisiana politician who advocated the redistribution of wealth and popularized the slogan 'Every Man a King'. He was critical of the rich and big banks, and was a hero to many of the poor and working class in Louisiana.

Part of Stanley and Blanche's conflict derives from his immigrant background. Blanche repeatedly refers to him as a 'Polack', which is an insulting term. Blanche makes clear her low opinion of the Polish when, in Scene 1, she describes them as 'something like Irish, aren't they? [...] Only not so – highbrow?'. As there was much discrimination against the Irish at this time, the audience would quickly perceive this insult. Stella describes Stanley's friends as a 'mixed lot' *(Scene 1)* and Williams's play is unusual for its time in its depiction of the easy mingling of characters from various ethnic backgrounds.

American Dream the idea that every American, whatever his or her background, can achieve prosperity and success through hard work

Williams presents Stella as having adjusted surprisingly quickly to her change in status and her new surroundings, which would have initially been as foreign to her as they are to Blanche. She believes in Stanley, saying **'Stanley's the only one of his crowd that's likely to get anywhere'** *(Scene 3)*. However she bases this more on his personal drive, energy and physicality than on any **'genius'** he may possess. While Blanche's background is filled with poetry, dances and letters, Stanley's life is work, bowling, poker and Stella. Stella, for the most part, accepts Stanley's priorities and needs.

Activity 4

a) Look closely at Scene 4, from Blanche's line **'I am not being or feeling at all superior, Stella'**, to the end of the scene.

b) Then answer the question: To what extent is Blanche's sense of social superiority responsible for her ultimate downfall? Use examples from this scene and elsewhere in the play to support your ideas.

The South

Tennessee Williams was born in Mississippi, in the 'Deep South' of America, and he later remembered his southern childhood as idyllic. However, when he was seven, his family moved to the Midwest, where he was teased about his accent and felt like an outsider. Throughout his writing career, he constantly returned to the South as his inspiration. He spent much of his adult life in Key West, Florida.

The South has complex **connotations** for many artists. It was a place of great beauty with a strong sense of history, but its wealth was primarily built on its slave-owning past. The defining event of the South was the Civil War (1861–1865) in which over 600,000 soldiers lost their lives and the Southern Confederate Army was eventually defeated.

Belle Reve, the DuBois's family home, would be a remnant of the earlier pre-war age. Many families lost their wealth during the war, but Blanche also blames years of mismanagement when male relations **'exchanged the land for their epic fornications'** *(Scene 2)*.

Americans would be familiar with depictions of the South, particularly from the 1936 Margaret Mitchell book *Gone with the Wind* and the more

This promotional card for the film *New Orleans* shows the sounds, colours and atmosphere of the city in the 1940s

famous 1939 film based on it, in which Scarlett O'Hara, like Blanche, struggles through various deprivations to hold onto her estate, Tara. But unlike Blanche, Scarlett, through her single-minded determination, is largely successful.

New Orleans, where Williams lived after graduating from college, is the setting for *A Streetcar Named Desire*. It too is in the South, but unlike Laurel, which was a small manufacturing town, New Orleans is a buzzing, multi-ethnic urban port, with close ties to Europe. It is situated in Louisiana, a former French and Spanish colony, which sets itself apart from the other states by its use of a legal 'Napoleonic code', to which Stanley refers. This means that certain laws reflect the state's European roots, including laws involving inheritance and property. Throughout the play, Williams emphasizes the unique setting of New Orleans with his descriptions of its colours, scents, music and characters.

Activity 5

Read the excerpt below, which describes Williams's first impressions of New Orleans. Highlight any similarities to the New Orleans portrayed in the play.

In December 1938 Tom [Tennessee Williams] travelled by bus from St. Louis to New Orleans. He felt – or so it seemed retrospectively – as if he were 'a migratory bird going to a more congenial climate.' It was almost like arriving in a different country. A.J. Liebling has said New Orleans is less like the southernmost point of the United States than the northernmost point of Costa Rica. Tom was suddenly in a more lackadaisical society where little attention was paid to either **propriety** or punctuality. In contrast to the Garden District and other respectable uptown areas, the French Quarter, where he settled, was slummy and sexually permissive.

(Ronald Hayman, *Tennessee Williams*: *Everyone Else is an Audience*)

Activity 6

Use a table like the one below to compare your impressions of New Orleans in the play with those of Mississippi (including both Laurel and Belle Reve).

	New Orleans	Mississippi
Employment		
Population/characters		
Key quotations		

connotations ideas or feelings associated with something

propriety obeying conventional rules of behaviour

Cultural context

The war encouraged audiences to seek escapism and the 1940s are considered by many to be the golden age of Broadway musicals. However, some of those musicals, such as *Carousel, Oklahoma* and *South Pacific* mixed light-heartedness with darker, more serious messages about war, prejudice and loss.

Many playwrights at this time focused on the plight of the working man. One of the most influential 20th-century playwrights was Eugene O'Neill, whose expressionist play *The Hairy Ape* (1922) features a brutal ship's stoker called Yank who, like Stanley, is compared to a primate. In the play, O'Neill explores the exploitation of the industrial working class and how Yank yearns to bring down his oppressors. Another of O'Neill's plays *A Moon for the Misbegotten* opened the same year as *A Streetcar Named Desire*.

During this period, Arthur Miller was emerging as one of the greatest 20th-century playwrights and his play *All My Sons* also premiered in 1947. It established his reputation, which was confirmed by his masterpieces *Death of a Salesman* (1949) and *The Crucible* (1953). Miller was a more political writer than Williams, often concentrating on the moral choices a torn male protagonist must make within a flawed community. Like Williams, Miller's work benefited from the advent of **method acting**, which encouraged raw, naturalistic performances, and they both had important plays directed by Elia Kazan, one of the most esteemed directors of the age.

Going to the cinema was a popular entertainment. Many filmmakers were attempting to explore serious and controversial topics at this time, but they had to work within the strict censorship of the day. In 1947, the 'Best Picture' Academy Award winner was *Gentleman's Agreement*, about a reporter pretending to be Jewish in order to expose anti-Semitism. The movie was directed by Elia Kazan, who also directed the first stage production of *A Streetcar Named Desire* that same year. One of the stars of *Gentlemen's Agreement* was John Garfield, who was one of the new naturalistic working-class actors and a predecessor of method actors like Marlon Brando. Garfield was originally offered the role of Stanley in *A Streetcar Named Desire* but made so many contractual and financial demands that the role went to the relatively unknown Brando.

Marlon Brando as Stanley in the 1951 film

The 1940s saw the blossoming of many other major writing talents. The novelist Ernest Hemingway published his acclaimed *For Whom the Bell Tolls* in 1940. Hemingway explored themes of war, love, nature and freedom in a spare and much imitated style. Williams's friend, Carson McCullers, used her background as an inspiration for her **southern gothic** novels such as *The Heart is a Lonely Hunter* (1940) and *The Member of the Wedding* (1946). Some of Williams's own writing, with its focus on decaying, dysfunctional southern families and dark secrets, is also considered to fall within the southern gothic tradition.

> **method acting** a system of acting that came into prominence in the 1930s in which actors learn to connect emotionally with the characters they are playing in order to produce realistic and original performances
>
> **southern gothic** a genre of fiction set in a decayed, damaged South of the United States; the novels often focus on the grotesque, bizarre or macabre

Activity 7

Read Blanche's speech in Scene 1 beginning with **'I, I, *I* took the blows…'**. Then make a bullet point list of any examples which fit with the ideas about death, the macabre, decaying and the grotesque in southern gothic literature.

Writing about context

Understanding the context of the play will help you to write with more depth and insight. However, it is important that you don't simply bolt dates and facts onto your essay, but use relevant information to support and strengthen your ideas. Some context that might be relevant could include:

- the expected gender roles of the time and how these influence the actions of the characters
- the specific background of New Orleans as conveyed by Williams through stage directions and characterization
- the importance of the 'dying South' in understanding Blanche's character
- the aspects of the play and characters which would have been shocking to an audience in the 1940s
- how social class and education is used as a source of conflict in the play
- how American post-Second World War preoccupations are presented in the play
- how the mingling of different ethnicities and social classes is depicted in the play.

Although Tennessee Williams wrote both poetry and short stories, he found himself drawn to the potential of the theatre and was actively involved in the development, casting, rehearsals and production of his plays. Most of his plays experimented with form and were, in many ways, ground-breaking for their time. He also experimented with genre, combining tragic and comic elements, and challenging the audience's expectations of what makes a sympathetic protagonist.

Tragedy

Many critics consider *A Streetcar Named Desire* to be one of the finest examples of a modern tragedy. In a typical reading of the play as a tragedy, Blanche is the protagonist and tragic heroine, whose **tragic flaws** (her inability to face reality; her mental and emotional vulnerability) are exploited by her **antagonist**, Stanley, leading to her tragic downfall (her exile to an asylum). Her tenuous grasp on the truth means that when she does tell the truth about Stanley's rape of her, she is not believed (or the other characters choose not to believe her).

However, some critics and audiences disagree with this reading of the text. Some point to the use of comedy, especially in the early scenes, as suggesting a tone and atmosphere too uneven to be conducive to tragedy, perhaps even tipping the play into **tragi-comedy.** Others find Blanche's actions so unsympathetic as to be unworthy of a tragic protagonist: her past is sordid and her goal, to marry a man she doesn't truly love, is unattractive. Some go so far as to feel that it is Stanley who is the protagonist, fighting off the elitist, decadent falsehoods of the past, representing instead the vital new working man.

> **antagonist** a character who opposes the protagonist
>
> **tragic flaw** a defect or failing in the tragic protagonist that brings around his or her downfall
>
> **tragi-comedy** a genre which includes aspects of both comedy and tragedy

The ancient Greek writer Aristotle defined tragedy as:

> '… the imitation of an action that is serious and also, having magnitude, complete in itself; in appropriate and pleasurable language […] in a dramatic rather than narrative form; with incidents arousing pity and fear, wherewith to accomplish a **catharsis** of these emotions.'
>
> (Aristotle, *The Poetics*, Part VI)

One issue some may have with the play is whether or not Blanche's actions are 'serious' and have the 'magnitude' or importance to qualify as a tragedy. However, it is clear that she feels herself to be involved in a life and death struggle, with ghosts from the past and images of death haunting the play.

Activity 1

a) Create a flow chart showing Blanche's journey through the play.

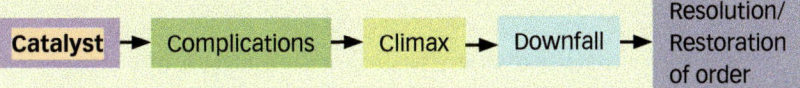

Catalyst → Complications → Climax → Downfall → Resolution/Restoration of order

b) Considering the information from this chapter, write a paragraph in response to the question: To what extent can *A Streetcar Named Desire* be considered a tragedy?

catalyst something or someone that starts or initiates an action or event

catharsis the purification or cleansing of emotion

Classical definitions of tragedy include the requirements of having a high-born hero (or, more rarely, heroine), e.g. a prince, king or general, who undertakes a momentous action which, in league with the protagonist's tragic flaw, leads to his downfall. The language spoken should be lofty and heightened, reflecting the consequence of the actions. So for example, in Shakespeare's *Macbeth,* which is written primarily in verse, the tragic hero Macbeth is a general. Due to Macbeth's tragic flaw of ambition he undertakes the momentous action of killing King Duncan, and subsequently is crowned king himself. He is consequently haunted by his actions and ultimately killed, with order restored by the arrival of Duncan's son Malcolm.

By the time of Tennessee Williams, many critics felt that classical tragedy was dead. They argued that the language of modern drama was too ordinary or the actions insignificant, and therefore it could not be regarded as true tragedy.

However, other critics believe that tragedy has changed in order to meet the demands of a new age and that the birth of modern tragedy was exemplified by the works of Arthur Miller and Tennessee Williams. Besides the sorrow which the audience might feel for the characters, there are other tragic factors, such as a preoccupation with death; being haunted by ghosts of the past; the raising and dashing of hopes; and the sense of the inevitability of the tragic ending. Some also look at the tragedy of a society, such as the dying hopes of the southern society in *A Streetcar Named Desire* or the blind superstitions of the witch-hunters in Arthur Miller's *The Crucible*.

It could be argued that Blanche's real tragic action, which occurred before the beginning of the play, was marrying Allan Grey and her subsequent denunciation of him. Therefore, the eleven scenes of *A Streetcar Named Desire* are simply the unspooling of this tragic mistake.

Activity 2

Read the following quotations about tragedy and note any connections you can make with the play A *Streetcar Named Desire*.

> Tragedy is only a way of assembling human misfortune, of **subsuming** it, and thus of justifying it by putting it into the form of a necessity, of a kind of wisdom, or of a purification.
>
> (Roland Barthes, quoted by Adrian Poole)

> The idea of a 'living death' looks like a modern complement to the old belief in ghosts, haunters, the revenants, the undead. It's a vision of death-in-life, a life so drained of meaning, value, purpose, and joy that it seems like death, being dead before you are dead.
>
> Yet in a broad sense, tragedy deals with toxic matter **bequeathed** by the past to the present. In personal terms, this often means what fathers and mothers have passed on to their children in the form of duties, loyalties, passions and injuries.
>
> (Adrian Poole, *Tragedy: A Very Short Introduction*)

bequeathed left in a will or handed down to a successor

subsuming including or absorbing

Activity 3

Use a table like the one below to locate some of the components of modern tragedy in *A Streetcar Named Desire*.

	Example	Quotations
Raising of hopes	Blanche hopes to marry Mitch.	'Sometimes – there's God – so quickly!' (Scene 6)
Dashing of hopes		
Past influencing the present		
Ghosts/haunting		
Death		
Following the fate of an individual and a community	Blanche represents the dying South.	

Comedy

It would be a very unconventional reading of the play to see it as a pure comedy. However, a few audiences have perceived Stanley as the hero of the play. Given that interpretation, they cheer his dominance over Blanche, laugh at his wisecracks and applaud the 'happy ending' with his wife and child. Williams, on the other hand, stated that his sympathies were with Blanche: '... it was Blanche whom I loved and respected and whom I wished to portray...' (quoted in *The World of Tennessee Williams*, edited by Richard F. Leavitt. W.H. Allen, London, 1978, page 77) and most productions respect these intentions. Nevertheless, there are undoubted comic elements in the play and it is a matter of interpretation to what extent they are given prominence.

Many classical tragedies include comic elements, such as the Porter's speech in *Macbeth*, the Fool's jokes in *King Lear* or the Nurse in *Romeo and Juliet*. These interludes can serve many purposes, including:

- momentarily releasing tension
- providing a contrast to the momentous events happening
- creating interest for the audience by altering the rhythm and mood of a scene.

The academic Adrian Poole argues that comedy within a tragedy should not simply be thought of as 'comic relief' but as a 'vital component of dramatic form':

 Most drama, except the very short, retains our attention by variations of tempo, mood, texture, focus, or perspective, for which the implied analogies with music and the visual arts are helpful. As a local effect, a comic voice or scene assists the whole rhythm by heightening and lowering tension.

(Adrian Poole, *Tragedy: A Very Short Introduction*)

 Activity 4

Read the quotations below. Identify when they occur and their comic effect.

- **What is this sister of yours, a deep-sea diver who brings up sunken treasures? Or is she the champion safe-cracker of all time!** *(Scene 2)*
- **Honey, would I be here if the man weren't married?** *(Scene 4)*
- **[*brightly*]: Did he *kill* her?** *(Scene 5)*
- **God *damn*, but that was a short day!** *(Scene 8)*

There is also a performance element in some of the humour. In the first scene, Eunice and the Negro Woman serve as an audience for Stanley's meat-throwing. They laugh and make light-hearted remarks to highlight a possibly crude interpretation of the action. In Scene 3, Steve tells his fellow poker players a **ribald** racist joke, which contrasts with their relative silence once Stella and Blanche – who presumably would be an unappreciative audience – enter. In Scene 8, Blanche rallies her performance skills to tell a joke to an unimpressed Stanley. In Scene 10, Stanley begins what, at first, seems to be a joke about his cousin who was a 'human bottle-opener' but it ends sourly with the ominous line, 'After that he was so ashamed of himself he used t' sneak out of the house when company came' (Scene 10).

Blanche (Jessica Lange) sprays perfume over Stanley (Toby Stephens) in the 1992 revival

Activity 5

Read the description below of Tallulah Bankhead's interpretation of Blanche in the 1956 New York revival of the play, which the influential critic Brooks Atkinson said was 'fundamentally comic' (quoted in Philip C. Kolin, *Williams: A Streetcar Named Desire*). Then compare it to the versions of the play or film you have seen.

For Bankhead, Blanche's humour was more than relief; it reflected her charm, sacred and **profane** at the same time. That humour, radically departing from the Blanches of Tandy, Hagen or Leigh [three actresses who had played the role on stage in early productions], emancipated Williams's script from stylized rigidity and encouraged audiences to discover another secret about Blanche not foregrounded in earlier productions.

(Philip C. Kolin, *Williams: A Streetcar Named Desire*)

Tragi-comedy

One can't write a tragedy today without putting humour into it. There has to be humour in it now; it's so hard for people to take tragedy seriously because people are so wary now.

(Tennessee Williams, in 1974 interview)

While a few radical re-workings of the play have concentrated on the comic elements, more productions have explored the poignant mixture of comedy and tragedy in it. For example, the comic courting between Blanche and Mitch, when he lifts her to guess her weight, is followed by Blanche's heartrending admission about her tragic marriage. Blanche's parrot joke precedes the violent clearing of the table by Stanley and her subsequent humiliation.

Williams was influenced by playwrights, like Anton Chekhov (1860–1904), who combined comedy and tragedy in their plays. Many audiences feel this mixture offers the most believable and realistic version of life. Chekhov's play *The Cherry Orchard* is about an aristocratic family who, due to their own inactivity and impracticality, lose their family estate to the son of a former servant, whose first action is to chop down their prized cherry orchard. Chekhov saw the play as a comedy, but the play's original director, Constantin Stanislavski focused on the more tragic elements. Critics have pointed out the similarities between Chekhov's aristocratic characters' futile efforts to save their estate and Blanche's loss of Belle Reve, as well as noting the ascendency of a new social class.

Realism and expressionism

Realism is a theme of the play with Mitch, in Scene 9, arguing for it and Blanche declaring that she desires **'magic'** instead. Realism is also a genre of theatre which encourages believable reproductions of life on stage. In terms of approaching a production of the play, a director must consider how he or she will convey both the realism and the magic Williams requires in it. **Expressionism**, which uses more stylized techniques, is one way of achieving this 'magic'.

expressionism a 20th-century movement which sought to express emotional experiences in a symbolic, distorted, stylized fashion

profane irreverent; disrespectful

realism presenting life or events without artificiality, aiming for truthfulness

ribald crude humour, usually involving jokes about sex

With the advent of method acting, as well as the influence of the cinema on the theatre, there was frequently an expectation in the mid-20th century that stage performances of serious, dramatic plays would be realistic. The stage directions of *A Streetcar Named Desire* suggest that Williams envisaged the production to be both realistic, with specific props and believable costumes, and expressionistic, with the use of shadows, sound effects and music to expose Blanche's emotional state.

There are also stage directions which can be ambiguous. For example, is the blue piano which *'expresses the spirit of the life which goes on here'* *(Scene 1)* simply the music that can be heard from the nearby nightclub, or is it representative of the influence of Stanley and New Orleans? Does the Mexican flower-seller exist or is she a figment of Blanche's imagination, signalling her fear of death?

Although interested in psychological realism, it is important to note that Williams also looked at symbolic, poetic and stylized ways of conveying his characters. Additionally, directors and designers may choose to either emphasize the realism of the production or to offer something more expressionistic. For example, the 2009 Donmar Warehouse production externalized Blanche's mental state by having her husband and lover appear on stage as ghostly figures who haunt her. A 2015 minimalist production at the Lyric Hammersmith had an institutional feeling with its bare white walls furnished with little besides a pile of luggage and scattered balloons.

The revolving set of the 2014 Young Vic production emphasized that Blanche was always on view

Tips for assessment

When writing about genre, remember to discuss those elements of the play which conform to a genre, as well as those which don't. This will show that you understand genre conventions and how a dramatist may mix genres or interpret them in an original way.

Activity 6

a) Look at the stage directions below and put them under the heading of either 'Realistic' or 'Expressionistic'.

- *There are vivid slices of watermelon on the table, whisky bottles, and glasses. (Scene 3)*

- *After a moment Stanley comes out of the bathroom dripping water and still in his clinging wet polka dot drawers. (Scene 3)*

- *Polka music sounds, in a minor key faint with distance. (Scene 6)*

- *The distant piano goes into a hectic breakdown. (Scene 7)*

- *He hurls a plate to the floor. (Scene 8)*

- *Lurid reflections appear on the walls around Blanche. The shadows are of a grotesque and menacing form. (Scene 10)*

- *The greeting is echoed and re-echoed by other mysterious voices behind the walls, as if reverberated through a canyon of rock. (Scene 11)*

b) Complete the following sentence: Williams uses expressionistic devices to convey…

Many see Williams's work as balancing different forms, with the conventions of the past set against a startling modernism. Some viewers feel that the casting in the film of *A Streetcar Named Desire* represented Williams's conflicting stylistic demands: Vivien Leigh, a renowned classical English actress and famous for appearing as the quintessential southern belle Scarlett O'Hara in the film *Gone With the Wind*, was cast against the raw, up-and-coming American method actor, Marlon Brando.

Writing about genre

When writing about the genre of the play, remember to do the following:

- Write about the play as a play, not a novel or story.
- Use the correct terminology, such as 'realism' or 'tragi-comedy'.
- Be sensitive to the different shadings and nuances of the play when a comic moment might be followed by a tragic one, and what this might show.
- Be aware of the different ways in which the play can be interpreted.
- Use your understanding of genre to analyse aspects of the play, such as its ending.

Main characters

Blanche DuBois

Blanche DuBois is considered one of the most complex and demanding roles in theatre. Tallulah Bankhead, who played the role in the 1956 New York revival, declared it was 'harder than 18 *King Lears* with a *Hamlet* thrown in' (reported to W. Hawkins, 1956). Rarely offstage, she must carry the audience through the play, exhibiting her many faults, while maintaining the integrity of the character.

Although Blanche is deceptive about her age, deflecting questions about it and, in Scene 3, claiming that Stella, her younger sister, is **'somewhat older than I'**, the stage directions in Scene 1 suggest she is **'about five years older than Stella'**, which would make her around 30. In Scene 5, Blanche nervously confesses that men **'lose interest quickly. Especially when the girl is over – thirty.'** The hesitation before the word 'thirty' highlights her discomfort. For Blanche's birthday cake, Stella cautiously stops at 25 candles, knowing that this is a sensitive subject. Although Blanche is not old, her fear of growing old alone and becoming an **'old maid'** is one of her key motivations. She refers to herself as a **'girl'** and avoids harsh lighting to hide her age, while hoping to marry Mitch as the most suitable of Stanley's acquaintances since she perceives this as a last chance at a fresh start.

The audience learns that Blanche married young, at 16, and there are suggestions that the young Blanche, although always **'flighty'** was very different from the damaged creature of the play. Stella describes how Blanche adored her young husband before discovering, in Stella's words, that he was **'a degenerate'**. After his death, Blanche's illusions were **'killed'** *(Scene 7)*. Blanche returned to her maiden name, DuBois, and looked after their dying relations, while Stella escaped to New Orleans. Blanche worked as a schoolteacher and remnants of her love of literature are evident in her references to poetry and her use of language.

Blanche, played by Gillian Anderson in the 2014 Young Vic production

Blanche clings to the social order in which she was born, expecting to be the centre of attention at social gatherings and the recipient of gallant behaviour from men. However, she also rebels against these conventions with her affairs with younger men, such as her young student and the soldiers in Laurel, as well as her stolen kiss with the Young Man in Scene 5. She is at once prim and flirtatious, innocent and knowing.

Although Tennessee Williams expressed great sympathy for Blanche, audiences sometimes reject her, judging her pretensions, aspirations and prejudices harshly. Jessica Tandy, the original Blanche, wrote to Williams, explaining the difficulty of being true to the finer aspects of Blanche and in portraying her tragedy in the face of the audience's increasing insensitivity. Williams, in turn, praised Tandy's unwavering understanding of the character.

> **Key quotation**
>
> **'You didn't know Blanche as a girl. Nobody, nobody, was tender and trusting as she was. But people like you abused her, and forced her to change.'** *(Stella, Scene 8)*

A key element of Blanche's character is her play-acting. Although audiences may judge her for her lack of truthfulness about her drinking, her age and her past, there is also a sense that pretence has become part of her nature: the role of a southern belle, one that she was brought up to play, even in as absurd a setting as the modest Kowalski apartment. After the dismal date with Mitch, she mourns that she **'couldn't rise to the occasion'** despite deserving **'ten points for trying'**. When Mitch asks her why she tried, she says she is observing the law of nature that **'the lady must entertain the gentleman'** *(Scene 6)*.

Activity 1

Read the critic's opinion below and then make a bullet point list of any examples in the play you can find when Blanche is 'performing'.

 A number of critics have analyzed Blanche in **metatheatrical** terms: she is an artist who dramatizes herself as if she were a stage character, playing roles detached from the reality of her situation, costuming herself from the trunk containing fake furs and costume jewelry, designing the lighting effects that will show her to advantage. With Mitch as her enthralled audience, she adds musical underscoring: she turns on the radio and 'waltzes to the music with romantic gestures'.

(Felicia Hardison Londre, 'A streetcar running fifty years', *The Cambridge Companion to Tennessee Williams*)

metatheatrical drawing attention to the theatricality of a performance, e.g. having a play-within-a play or a character overtly play-acting; drawing attention to the artificiality of a performance

Activity 2

Blanche is a character with whom the audience's sympathy may vary from scene to scene or even moment to moment. Use a table like the one below to begin noting when you feel sympathetic towards Blanche and when you feel annoyed, angry or frustrated by her. Your reaction is personal and may be different to that experienced by others.

Key moment	Your reaction	Explanation
Scene 1: Blanche's conversation with Eunice	Not entirely sympathetic	She seems rude to Eunice, who is trying to be helpful and friendly. ('I'd like to be left alone.')
Scene 1: Blanche's description of the loss of Belle Reve		
Scene 3: First conversation with Mitch		
Scene 4: Complaints about Stanley		
Scene 6: Description of Allan Grey's death		
Scene 10: Fight with Stanley		
Scene 11: Her exit		

Stanley Kowalski

Stanley is Blanche's antagonist, who ultimately brings about her downfall. However, he is not a simple villain and audiences may find themselves sympathizing with or attracted to him. Williams wrote about being divided between 'the raw, sensual, dynamic', which Stanley could be said to represent, and the more 'delicate' and 'finer' aspects of the play, as portrayed by Blanche. It is Stanley's world, with its bright colours, jazz music and physical dynamism into which Blanche has intruded.

Stanley (Alec Baldwin) and Stella (Diane Lane) in the 1995 TV play

At first, there is some sense of this being a **comedy of manners**, where Stanley's unselfconscious masculinity collides with Blanche's elaborate feminine artifice. His first action of the play, throwing the meat to Stella, signals what an unusual and 'raw' character he is – even in the accepting environment of Elysian Fields, it is commented on by Eunice and the Negro Woman.

comedy of manners a play which mocks the social behaviour of a particular group

Activity 3

Throughout the play, Stanley is in motion, constantly reasserting his physical dominance. Look at the actions from the first three scenes in the table below and analyse what you learn about his character.

Actions	Analysis
Scene 1: Bowling/Throwing meat/Getting whisky bottle/ Taking off shirt	He is unselfconscious, unafraid to draw attention to himself...
Scene 2: Going through Blanche's wardrobe trunk/Kicks trunk closed/Lights a cigarette/Takes Blanche's atomizer/ Goes through trunk/Snatches letters	
Scene 3: Playing cards/Tosses watermelon rinds on the floor/Whacks Stella/Turns off radio/Throws radio out of the window/Offstage 'the sound of a blow'/He falls on his knees on the steps/ Lifts her off her feet	

Key quotation

'Animal joy in his being is implicit in all his movements and attitudes.' (Scene 1)

Stanley is the son of Polish immigrants, proud now to be 'one hundred per cent American' *(Scene 8)*. Although he admits he was not a 'very good English student' *(Scene 1)*, he has progressed from being a master sergeant in the Engineers' Corps to a travelling salesman, and Stella has hopes that he will be promoted further. He takes pride in having 'pulled' Stella 'down off them columns' despite being 'common as dirt' *(Scene 8)*. His anger at overhearing Blanche's criticisms of him leads him to plan her return to Laurel.

Activity 4

a) Read John Lahr's comment on the character of Stanley.

> Part of Stanley's sexual charge is the wallop of his selfishness, which registered the spiritual shift after America's return to normalcy. 'He builds a hedonistic life, and fights to the death to defend it,' Kazan wrote about him in his notebooks. Liberated from duty, from sacrifice, from class restrictions – all the emotional baggage that Blanche brings with her, represented by the loss of the family plantation, the well-named Belle Reve – each character pursues his own creaturely self-interest.
>
> (John Lahr, *Tennessee Williams: Mad Pilgrimage of the Flesh*)

b) Write a paragraph answering the question: To what extent does Stanley represent post-Second World War America?

Stella Kowalski

Stella is the bridge between the world of the Kowalskis and the DuBoises. Although presumably raised similarly to Blanche, she appears to have escaped the demands of her family and settled with relative ease into her new life in New Orleans.

Stella speaks much less than Blanche, which Blanche comments on: **'How quiet you are, you're so peaceful'** (*Scene 1*). Williams's stage directions indicate that she understands her sister, for whom her feelings are both fond and exasperated. She panders to Blanche's vanity and, without success, encourages Stanley to do the same. She is then in the awkward position of trying to make peace between her warring husband and sister.

Stella, played by Kim Hunter in the 1951 film, with Marlon Brando as Stanley

Activity 5

a) Williams provides many clues in his stage directions as to how he believes Stella should be played. Look at the examples below and make notes on what they reveal about Stella.

   i. *She cries out in protest but manages to catch it: then she laughs breathlessly. (Scene 1)*

   ii. *Stella looks up with a radiant smile. (Scene 1)*

   iii. *Her eyes go blind with tenderness as she catches his head and raises him level with her. (Scene 3)*

   iv. *Her eyes and lips have that almost narcotized tranquillity that is in the faces of Eastern idols. (Scene 4)*

   v. *Stella has embraced him with both arms, fiercely, and full in the view of Blanche. (Scene 4)*

b) From the above evidence and other examples from the play, answer the question: What do we learn about Stella's relationship with Stanley from the stage directions provided by Williams?

There are two key moments when Stella needs to choose between her husband and her sister. The first is in Scene 4, when she ignores Blanche's exhortations to leave Stanley, and the second, and more devastating, is when she chooses to believe Stanley rather than accept Blanche's version of what happened between them the night she was in hospital. Ultimately her loyalty to her husband, as well as the security he provides for her and their child, outweighs her belief in Blanche. Knowing her sister's need for **'magic'**, she presents Blanche's banishment to what is most likely a rudimentary state asylum (**'the unmistakable aura of the state institution with its cynical detachment'**) as a **'rest in the country'** *(Scene 11)*. She feels guilty about this, sobbing with **'inhuman abandon'** at Blanche's exit, but is then consoled by physical contact with Stanley: **'The luxurious sobbing, the sensual murmur fade away'** *(Scene 11)*.

Tips for assessment

Upgrade

To make sure you are writing about the characters as constructions of the author rather than real people, try to use phrases like 'Williams presents Blanche as…' or 'In contrast to Blanche, Williams shows Stella to be…'.

Harold Mitchell (Mitch)

To Blanche, Mitch stands out from Stanley's friends as being **'superior to the others'** *(Scene 3)*. An old army friend of Stanley's, he now works on the **'precision bench in the spare parts department'** for the same company where Stanley works *(Scene 3)*. Williams may have intended a certain irony in Mitch's job title: 'precision' could suggest the more delicate and **'sensitive'** emotions Blanche attributes to him, but he is also, like Blanche, a 'spare part'. In a world of couples, they are alone and isolated, drained by their time spent looking after elderly and ill relations. He says to his poker friends about his mother, **'You all are married. But I'll be alone when she goes'** *(Scene 3)*, highlighting his separateness.

Mitch, played by Karl Malden in the 1951 film

In Scene 3, his gentle attraction to Blanche is clear, though their first meeting is the very unromantic setting of his trip to the bathroom. Williams describes him as acting *'a little shyly'* and giving *'an embarrassed laugh'*. Later in that scene, when Blanche dances, he is *'delighted and moves in awkward imitation like a dancing bear'* *(Scene 3)*.

His innocence and sincerity sets him apart from the other characters and in Scene 6 he offers hope to Blanche: **'You need somebody. And I need somebody, too. Could it be – you and me, Blanche?'**

This scene contrasts with his cruelty in Scene 9, when he undertakes one of the most iconic actions in the play, shining the naked light onto Blanche's face. While her confession of her young husband's death in Scene 6 brings Mitch closer to her, her admission in Scene 9 of her affairs with the young soldiers is the final break in their relationship. When he tries to embrace her, it is an act of vengeance rather than love, a settling of a bill for a summer's attentions.

In the final scene, Mitch is presented as a broken man. Although he is again seated at the poker table, his anger towards Stanley **'I'll kill you!'** is a far cry from the previously gentle Mitch. The last specific stage direction referring to Mitch shows his desperation *'Mitch collapses at the table, sobbing'* *(Scene 11)* suggesting that it is not just Blanche's life which has been permanently blighted, but his as well.

Key quotations

'Poker should not be played in a house with women.' *(Scene 3)*

'She wants me to be settled down before she –' *(Scene 6)*

'I don't mind you being older than what I thought. But all the rest of it – God! [...] I was a fool enough to believe you was straight.' *(Scene 9)*

'You're not clean enough to bring in the house with my mother.' *(Scene 9)*

 Activity 6

Use a table like the one below to trace the trajectory of Mitch's relationship with Blanche in the play.

	Relationship to Blanche	Key quotations
Scene 3		
Scene 6		
Scene 9		
Scene 11		

In his notebook, the original director of the play, Elia Kazan, wrote about each of the character's 'masks' (what they present to the world) and 'spines' (what motivates them). He noted that Blanche's mask was a 'Damsel in Distress' but that her spine was to 'find protection'. He thought that Mitch presented himself as a 'He-Man Mama's Boy' but that his true motivation was to get away from his mother.

 Activity 7

Using Kazan's idea explained above, complete a table like the one below with what *you* believe are the external 'masks' of the characters and their internal 'spines' or motivations.

Mask	Character	Spine
	Blanche	
	Stanley	
	Stella	
	Mitch	

Tips for assessment

Every character in a play has a function – a reason that the playwright included them. You will need to show that you understand the function of a character within any character analysis.

Minor characters

Eunice Hubbel

Eunice and her husband Steve are the upstairs neighbours of the Kowalskis. She is first described as the **'white woman'** who is speaking to her black neighbour, as an early indication of the **'easy intermingling of races in the old part of town'** *(Scene 1)*. She is a typical good neighbour, letting Stella's sister into the Kowalski apartment; providing a refuge for Stella when she escapes from Stanley in Scene 3; and, in Scene 11, comforting Stella and being kind to Blanche.

Her relationship with Steve is at times tempestuous. In Scene 5 they can be heard fighting (**'Eunice's voice shouts in terrible wrath'**), which leads to Blanche's humorous, **'Did he *kill* her?'** Eunice is jealous of the time Steve spends away from her and accuses him of chasing a **'blonde'**. She is quick to threaten to call the police or vice squad, whether it be for Steve's actions in Scene 5 or Stanley's in Scene 3. However, there is no evidence of her actually contacting the police, instead preferring to get a drink. The fights between Steve and Eunice seem to be part of the fabric of life in New Orleans and more a source of humour than concern to their neighbours.

In the final scene, Eunice provides practical help to Stella, acting as her confidante and helping her with Blanche. Some critics have noted a resemblance in her lines of encouragement to Stella to Sonya's at the end of Chekhov's *Uncle Vanya*, who says:

> What can we do? We must live out our lives. [*A pause*] Yes, we shall live, Uncle Vanya. We shall live all through the endless procession of days ahead of us, and through the long evenings. We shall bear patiently the burdens that fate imposes on us.
>
> (Anton Chekhov, *Uncle Vanya*)

Activity 8

One interpretation of the Hubbels is that they represent what Stanley and Stella are going to become. Make a bullet point list of the similarities between the Hubbels and Kowalskis.

Steve Hubbel

Steve, Eunice's husband, is the poker-playing and bowling neighbour of the Kowalskis. A less dominant character than Stanley, he is still intent on pursuing his interests to his wife's irritation. However, unlike Stanley and Stella, the Hubbels seem to be a more even match. Eunice throws things at him and tells him to get his own food as she won't cook for him when she's angry. One stage direction says that he has a *'bruise on his forehead'*, presumably from something Eunice has hurled at him and later that he looks to see if Eunice is there *'a bit timidly'*, showing that he is not the undisputed 'king' of his household *(Scene 5)*.

In the poker night scene *(Scene 3)*, which he opens with the line *'Anything wild this deal?'*, he tells a joke which serves as a comic counterpoint to Stanley's increasing anger. In the hierarchy of the poker players, he is subservient to Stanley, but joins with the others to tease Mitch. He helps the other men in calming down Stanley by putting him under the shower, then beats a hasty retreat, pausing only to gather up his winnings.

In the final scene, he is again playing poker, but this time Stanley is winning and Steve is largely silent. He restrains the angry Mitch at one point and utters the final line of the play: *'This game is seven-card stud'* *(Scene 11)*.

Activity 9

Look closely at the two poker scenes and decide the hierarchy of the players from 1 (being the most powerful) to 4 (least powerful). Supply quotations to support your point of view.

Pablo Gonzales

Pablo, who plays poker with Stanley, Mitch and Steve, provides another example of the multiculturalism of the New Orleans neighbourhood. The poker players are described in the stage directions as being *'men at the peak of their physical manhood, as coarse and direct and powerful as the primary colours'* (Scene 3). At one point Pablo suggests they get some **'chop suey'**, a blended American-Chinese dish, another example of the blending of cultures.

In the final scene, he speaks in Spanish, provoking an angry and insulting, **'Put it in English, greaseball'** from Stanley. His *'Maldita sea tu suerto!'* (damn your luck) refers to Stanley's luck at cards, but Stanley's *'prodigiously elated'* reaction might indicate that he is also lucky that Blanche is leaving their home. Later in the scene, Pablo pronounces in both English and Spanish what a **'bad thing'** is happening to Blanche *(Scene 11)*.

The poker game in the Donmar Warehouse production, 2009 (Pablo, Stanley, Steve and Mitch, from left to right)

Activity 10

Write a paragraph explaining how the presence of the poker players adds to the **pathos** of the last scene.

Negro Woman

In the first scene, the Negro Woman helps to establish the informal and friendly attitude of the inhabitants of Elysian Fields. In the 1940s, 'negro' or 'coloured' would be considered an acceptable way of describing an African-American (whereas the term 'nigger' used by Steve in his Scene 3 joke was a derogatory term, in the same way that 'Polack' is insulting to Stanley). However, it is worth noting that unlike Eunice, the Negro Woman is not given a name. Her opening lines create the impression that the audience is catching the characters mid-conversation and provide a certain mystery. She then advises a sailor about the Four Deuces, the local nightclub, claiming it is a **clip joint** that sells strong cocktails.

In Scene 5, the Negro Woman comes *'drunkenly'* out of the very club against which she'd warned the sailor and says something suggestive to the Young Man (*she *'snaps her fingers before his belt'*, but *'The Young Man shakes his head violently...'*).

Her primary role is to add to the atmosphere of Elysian Fields, which contrasts with Blanche's expectations. Her final appearance is a brief interlude in Scene 10, shortly before Blanche's rape, when she is seen *'rooting excitedly'* through the sequined bag which a prostitute has dropped. This could be read as a foreshadowing of the stealing of the last of Blanche's self-esteem and sanity or the breaking down of social norms.

> **clip joint** a bar or nightclub which deceptively overcharges for drinks
>
> **pathos** encouraging feelings of sorrow and pity

A Strange Man (Doctor)

In Scene 11, the Doctor and Matron arrive. They are described as having the *'aura of the state institution with its cynical detachment'*. However, later in the scene the Doctor *'becomes personalized'* and the *'inhuman quality goes'* *(Scene 11)*. He reads Blanche's character well and understands that she will respond to gentleness. In her mind, he becomes a gentleman caller and she holds *'tight to his arm'* *(Scene 11)*. Her words to him, *'Whoever you are – I have always depended on the kindness of strangers'* *(Scene 11)*, echo the words she utters to Mitch at the end of Scene 3 about the importance of 'kindness'.

> **Key quotation**
>
> *She allows him to lead her as if she were blind. (Scene 11)*

A Strange Woman (Nurse), or Matron

Unlike the doctor, the matron does not undergo a change but remains a symbol of the harsh new reality which faces Blanche. She is the **antithesis** of Blanche, described as a *'heavy woman'* and a *'peculiarly sinister figure in her severe dress'* *(Scene 11)*. Although not overtly cruel, she represents the realism from which Blanche flinches.

Key quotation

These fingernails have to be trimmed. *(Scene 11)*

---

antithesis entirely opposite to something or someone

Activity 11

Answer the question: What is the dramatic function of the entrance of the Doctor and Matron?

A Young Collector (Young Man)

The innocent youth of the Young Man contrasts with the desperate hopes of the older Blanche and Mitch. The Young Man arrives to collect for the newspaper delivery and immediately interests Blanche. Blanche emphasizes his youth, not only by repeating the word **'young'** six times, but also her teasing comments about his **'cherry soda'**. She then, after kissing him, says she must keep her **'hands off children'** *(Scene 5)*.

Key quotations

'Has anyone ever told you that you look like a young prince out of the Arabian Nights?' *(Blanche, Scene 5)*

'Don't you just love these long rainy afternoons in New Orleans when an hour isn't just an hour – but a little bit of Eternity dropped in your hands – and who knows what to do with it?' *(Blanche, Scene 5)*

Dramatically, the Young Man serves several purposes: he foreshadows Blanche's revelations about her past with both her husband and her student, but also serves as a contrast to Mitch's arrival seconds after he has disappeared. With him, the audience sees a different side to Blanche, in which she is confident and seductive.

Activity 12

Complete a table like the one below comparing Blanche's behaviour in Scene 5 with the Young Man and in Scene 6 with Mitch.

	Scene 5	Scene 6
Examples of physical proximity		
Reaction to kisses		
Flirtatious behaviour		
Dialogue		

A Mexican Woman

The Mexican Woman is a mysterious figure who appears in Scene 9 selling flowers for the dead. She is described as blind and wearing a dark shawl. She carries bunches of tin flowers, which are typically displayed at Mexican funerals. Her words foreshadow the play's impending tragedy, as well as Blanche's preoccupation with death (mysteriously, at the end of Scene 8, Blanche begins whispering in Spanish). The Mexican Woman is a ghostly figure speaking *'barely audibly'* and only *'faintly visible' (Scene 9)*. She may be a subtle reference to Tiresias, a blind prophet in Greek tragedies.

Writing about characters

When writing about characters and characterization, remember to do the following:

- Discuss the characters as characters rather than as real people.
- Consider the different ways a character could be interpreted.
- Think about the character's role and function in the play.
- Reflect on the character's importance to the play as a whole.
- Analyse the character's development throughout the play.
- Consider not only what the character says and does, but how other characters perceive him or her.
- Note any insights into the characters provided by Williams's stage directions.
- Reflect on how the context of the play may influence how characters are understood.

Williams's distinctive use of lyrical dialogue, symbolic imagery and muscular dramatic action are distinctive features of *A Streetcar Named Desire*. From the beginning of the play, with its intriguing title, poetic **epigraph** and detailed, atmospheric stage directions, the unique voice and concerns of the playwright are established.

> **epigraph** a quotation at the beginning of a literary work which indicates the concerns or themes that will follow

Epigraph

Williams was a great admirer of the work of poet Hart Crane (1899–1932) and chose for his epigraph the fifth stanza of Crane's lyrical poem, 'The Broken Tower', which was written in 1932 only months before Crane's suicide. The poem itself has been interpreted in many ways, but the stanza chosen for Williams's epigraph suggests several connections to the play. The images in the poem succeed in evoking the delicate, fractured, melancholy world of Blanche as she seeks 'the visionary company of love'.

Activity 1

a) Use a table like the one below to analyse possible interpretations of key quotations from the poem in relation to the play.

b) Then answer the question: How does the epigraph suggest the themes of *A Streetcar Named Desire*?

Quotation	Connection to themes of *A Streetcar Named Desire*
'broken world'	Could mean the world of Elysian Fields which Blanche is entering or a world broken by war. Blanche herself is broken, as is the world she is escaping in the South.
'visionary company of love'	
'An instant in the wind'	
'I know not whither hurled'	
'not for long to hold each desperate choice'	

Stage directions

Compared to many 21st-century playwrights, Williams's stage directions are unusually detailed and poetic. They do far more than simply indicate the appearance of a scene or character, but often go to lengths to establish the atmosphere in language which is more lyrical and evocative than usual. Audiences seeing the play would not get the full benefit of these stage directions, but they provide the reader and theatre practitioners with an insight into Williams's ideas about the characters and settings.

Activity 2

a) Look at the stage directions at the opening of the play, starting with *'The exterior of a two-storey corner building'* and ending with *'the voices of people on the street can be heard overlapping'* *(Scene 1)*, noting any directions you think would be specifically helpful to the director or designer of the play.

b) Next highlight any which you believe are only useful to the reader.

c) Lastly, imagine you were the designer of the play and complete the following sentence: 'From the opening stage directions, my chief goals would be to...'

Activity 3

The stage directions also provide indications of how Williams would like specific characters or moments to be played.

a) Test your knowledge of the character and stage directions by assigning the correct character to each of the following stage directions.

   i. *Then he jerks open a small drawer in the trunk and pulls up a fistful of costume jewellery. (Scene 2)*

   ii. *She sprays herself with her atomizer; then playfully sprays him with it. (Scene 2)*

  iii. *Her face is serene in the early morning sunlight. (Scene 4)*

  iv. *_____ and _____ come around the corner. _____'s arm is around _____'s shoulder and she is sobbing luxuriously and he is cooing love-words. (Scene 5)*

   v. *_____ clears his throat and looks glancingly at the door. (Scene 5)*

  vi. *_____ cackling hysterically, swaying drunkenly, comes around the corner from the Four Deuces. (Scene 5)*

 vii. *_____ is bearing, upside down, a plaster statuette of Mae West... (Scene 6)*

b) Explain what each stage direction reveals about the character.

Dialogue

Dialogue is the primary tool of the playwright. Williams ensures that his characters are vividly conveyed by his character-specific dialogue, which is coloured by their backgrounds, desires and emotional states.

In the opening scene, the rhythms of New Orleans are captured in the snatches of dialogue: two women chatting, a lost sailor asking directions, a vendor shouting. This is followed by a short section of dialogue between Stanley and Mitch, which through the use of **sociolect**, indicates their working-class status. Words like **'naw'**, **'gotta'** and even **'Baby'** introduce Stanley's rough-hewn background. Stanley's dialogue is direct, such as the monosyllabic command **'Catch!'**, followed by an equally short explanation, **'Meat!'**. Blanche's dialogue provides a contrast to Stanley's, as she **'with faintly hysterical humour'** flutters through a description of her journey *(Scene 1)*. The use of dashes in her dialogue reflects her tendency to hesitate or break off sentences.

Blanche's **diction** indicates her upbringing with its wide vocabulary, whereas many of the residents of Elysian Fields use more informal language, with some, like Stanley, utilizing unconventional grammar (**'there wasn't no'** *(Scene 1)*, **'ain't I'** *(Scene 8)*). It can also be assumed that characters like Pablo speak in a **dialect** to reflect that English is not their first language. Characters may also change the **register** of their speaking depending upon their audience. For example, Stella speaks differently to Stanley than she does to Blanche and Blanche creates a new character for herself when imagining she is addressing Shep Huntleigh.

Activity 4

a) Read the examples of dialogue below and identify which character is speaking.

b) Analyse how specific uses of language are distinctive to that character.

  i. I am spending the summer on the wing, making flying visits here and there. *(Scene 5)*

  ii. Them darn mechanics at Fritz's don't know their can from third base! *(Scene 4)*

  iii. I am ashamed of the way I perspire. My shirt is sticking to me. *(Scene 6)*

  iv. I don't believe all of those stories and I think your supply-man was mean and rotten to tell them. It's possible that some of the things he said are partly true. *(Scene 7)*

  v. It's sort of messed up right now but when it's clean it's real sweet. *(Scene 1)*

  vi. I am cursing your goddam luck. *(Scene 11)*

Imagery

Williams's writing is noted for its rich poetry and **imagery**, including his use of **figurative language**.

Animal imagery

Blanche (Glenn Close) arrives in a white outfit in the 2002 National Theatre production

One of the original titles of the play was *The Moth* and throughout the play Williams uses animal, bird or insect imagery to convey his characters. In Scene 1, Williams writes *'There is something about her uncertain manner, as well as her white clothes, that suggests a moth.'* This establishes not only Blanche's delicate nature but also her fatal relationship with light. Blanche herself uses imagery. For example, in Scene 5, she employs an extended **metaphor** about a bird in her letter to Shep Huntleigh: she is spending the summer *'on the wing'*, making *'flying visits'* and perhaps will *'swoop down on Dallas!'* These images suggest Blanche's restless energy and reinforce the idea of her being, as Stella puts it in Scene 7, *'flighty'*.

dialect pronunciations and word choices used by people of a particular geographical region

diction choice of words

figurative language a variety of literary techniques, such as metaphors and similes, which go beyond the literal meaning of words

imagery the use of visual or other vivid language to convey ideas or emotions

metaphor a figure of speech when two things are compared without using the word 'like' or 'as'

register use of language which changes in formality depending on the situation

sociolect pronunciations and word choices used by people of a particular social class

Activity 5

Explain how the imagery works in each of the examples below and note what each example suggests about the character.

i. *the power and pride of a richly feathered male bird among hens* *(about Stanley, Scene 1)*

ii. *you're just as plump as a little partridge* *(about Stella, Scene 1)*

iii. *Mitch is delighted and moves in awkward imitation like a dancing bear.* *(Scene 3)*

iv. *He acts like an animal, has an animal's habits! [...] Night falls and the other apes gather!* *(about Stanley, Scene 4)*

v. *Have got to be seductive – put on soft colours, the colours of butterfly wings, and glow* *(about Blanche, Scene 5)*

vi. *Tiger – tiger!* *(about Blanche, Scene 10)*

Tips for assessment

A Streetcar Named Desire is renowned for its rich language. You will be expected to comment on the variety of literary techniques and vocabulary Williams uses, and support your points with quotations. These do not always have to be long quotations – one or two words may be enough.

Colour imagery

One of the early suggested titles for the play was *Primary Colours* and, from the opening stage directions, Williams infuses the play with a vivid use of colour. Colours represent many things: the vibrancy of New Orleans; the physicality of the men; the sensuality of the women; and the fragility of Blanche.

Blanche's own name means 'white' in French, which is reinforced by her first costume, and she married a man whose last name was 'Grey'. She enters the play, *'daintily dressed in a white suit with a fluffy bodice'* *(Scene 1)* and, in the last scene, she chooses a jacket of **'Della Robbia blue'**. Her journey from a virginal white, via her *'dark red satin wrapper'* in Scene 3 to a blue that is reminiscent of a Madonna, traces the different stages of the audience's perception of her character. As she assumes the colour associated with the Virgin Mary, the audience can decide if this is ironic or if she has undergone a cleansing process, by which she has emerged renewed and pure.

Activity 6

Read the following examples of colour imagery and make notes on what they suggest about the characters and setting.

i. *The sky [...] is a peculiarly tender blue, almost turquoise* (Scene 1)

ii. *I like an artist who paints in strong, bold colours, primary colours. I don't like pinks and creams and I never cared for wish-washy people.* (Blanche, Scene 2)

iii. *The poker players [...] wear coloured shirts, solid blues, a purple, a red-and-white check, a light green* (Scene 3)

iv. *She has a tragic radiance in her red satin robe following the sculptural lines of her body.* (Scene 11)

v. *It's Della Robbia blue. The blue of the robe in the old Madonna pictures.* (Blanche, Scene 11)

vi. *And I'll be buried at sea sewn up in a clean white sack and dropped overboard – at noon – in the blaze of summer – and into an ocean as blue as [chimes again] my first lover's eyes.* (Blanche, Scene 11)

Activity 7

Read this student's attempt to write about the colours in the play. Put a tick for every point made and underline each supporting example. Then complete the paragraph in your own words.

In the play, Williams uses colours to emphasize Blanche's outsider status. In the opening scene, the vibrant and diverse nature of Elysian Fields is established partly through colours: 'the brown river', the 'tender blue' sky, as well as the music of the 'blue piano' and the multicultural neighbours, 'a white woman' and a 'coloured woman'. In contrast, Blanche's appearance in her white suit, 'dainty' and 'fluffy', is 'incongruous' as if she is going to attend 'a summer tea' or a 'cocktail party' rather than visiting this working-class neighbourhood, with its men in blue denim, who are throwing 'red-stained' packages to their wives. It is easy to imagine that her white clothes and gloves will quickly be soiled by her rough environment.

Allusions

Appropriate to her background as a cultured English teacher, Blanche's dialogue is littered with cultural and literary **allusions**. Some are overt, like her discussion with Mitch about the quotation by Elizabeth Barrett Browning in Scene 3, while others are more oblique. For example, her line to the Young Man in Scene 5, **'but a little bit of Eternity dropped in your hands'** probably alludes to a line in the poem 'Auguries of Innocence' by William Blake (1757–1827):

> To see a world in a grain of sand,
> And a heaven in a wild flower,
> Hold infinity in the palm of your hand,
> And eternity in an hour.
>
> (William Blake, 'Auguries of Innocence')

However, in Blanche's revised version, the possibilities of this unexpected hour have sensual or erotic overtones.

Other allusions in Scene 5 include her announcement that the Young Man is like a **'young prince out of the Arabian Nights'** and her greeting of Mitch as **'My Rosenkavalier!'** On the surface, both of these are highly unlikely comparisons, but also suggest Blanche's obsessions. 'Arabian Nights' refers to *One Thousand and One Nights*, in which a young virgin, Scheherazade, must enchant the king each night with a new tale or face death. Like Scheherazade, Blanche is a weaver of tales, who believes she must entertain men. 'Rosenkavalier' refers to the comic opera *Der Rosenkavalier* in which an older woman, the Marschalin, has a young lover who is asked to present a rose to the young fiancée of a baron. The two young characters fall in love, to the bittersweet disappointment of the Marschalin, who is left to ponder her own loss of youth. Although superficially Blanche's comment refers to the bunch of roses Mitch is carrying, it could also reflect Blanche's fascination with a younger man, which mirrors the Marschalin's. In both tales there is a collision of love and mortality.

> **allusion** a figure of speech which references the Bible, a myth or work of literature to comment upon something else

Complete a table like the one below with your notes of the listed allusions (you may need to look up some of the allusions on the internet).

Allusion	Context	What it means
'Only Poe! Only Mr Edgar Allan Poe! – could do it justice! Out there I suppose is the ghoul-haunted woodland of Weir!' (Scene 1)	This is Blanche's shocked reaction to Stella's apartment and environment.	Edgar Allan Poe was famous for writing eerie ghost tales. The last line is a direct quotation of a ballad by Poe where a lover wanders a bleak landscape, happening upon the tomb of his lost love. Blanche is not only saying how dismal Elysian Fields is, but may also be subconsciously referring to her own obsessions with death and the suicide of her husband.
'I attempt to instil a bunch of bobby-soxers and drug-store Romeos with reverence for Hawthorne and Whitman and Poe!' (Scene 3)		
'Je suis la Dame aux Camellias! Vous êtes – Armand! Understand French?' (Scene 6)		

Hyperbole

Blanche's self-dramatizing nature makes her inclined to **hyperbole**. Her reaction to Stella's modest apartment is an extravagant 'Never, never, never in my worst dreams could I picture…' and she describes the death of their relations by dramatically **personifying** death: 'Why, the Grim Reaper had put up his tent on our doorstep' (Scene 1).

However, it is not only Blanche who uses hyperbole. Stanley assesses Blanche's items of costume jewellery and outfits in hyperbolic terms as 'a solid-gold dress', 'Genuine fox fur-pieces, a half a mile long', 'Pearls! Ropes of them!' and 'A crown for an empress' (Scene 2). It is the realistic Stella who brings Stanley down to earth, explaining that the tiara is merely rhinestone, which is 'Next door to glass' (Scene 2). This scene shows how naïve Stanley is, unable to discern wealth from make-believe.

Similarly, Stella has to try to calm Blanche's hyperbolic excesses, e.g. laughing off her 'desperate' appeal to Shep Huntleigh with a 'Don't be so ridiculous, darling!' (Scene 4)

Blanche's and Stanley's excessive natures are exposed by their use of exaggeration.

hyperbole exaggeration

personifying giving human attributes to an idea or object

Symbolism

Williams uses **symbolism** to convey key themes in the play and to expose the characters' mental states. Examples of this include his use of water, light and the streetcar.

> **symbolism** representing something with something else, such as a cross to represent Christianity or chains to represent enslavement

Washing

Throughout the play, to Stanley's obvious annoyance, Blanche takes a series of baths to calm and refresh herself. For Blanche, washing represents renewal and a return to an earlier time. For Stanley, Blanche's use of the bathroom is part of a territorial war. He views her as monopolizing an essential part of his house, but also resents the way she orders Stella to wait on her during this ritual. It also heightens the sense of intimacy in the small apartment as Blanche is regularly in a state of undress, wrapped in towels or a robe.

From the bathroom, the others in the apartment can hear her singing songs. The first of these songs, in Scene 2, is a love song, which suggests Blanche's romantic nature, but also her view of herself as helpless, captive and a maiden. In Scene 7, she can be heard singing 'Paper Moon', a sweetly romantic 1930s song which focuses on magic and make-believe themes close to Blanche's heart. Blanche's cleansing ritual seems to return her to a long-ago innocence and she emerges saying, **'Oh, I feel so good after my long, hot bath, I feel so good and cool and – rested'** (Scene 7).

Dramatically, Blanche's trips to the bathroom are among the only times when she is off-stage and when other characters can discuss her, so there is often an irony in her feeling renewed and refreshed, while Stanley is plotting her removal.

The bathroom also plays an important role in bringing Mitch and Blanche together: **'I'm going to the "head". Deal me out'** (Scene 3). Mitch is self-conscious about meeting Blanche outside the bathroom when he **'realizes he still has the towel in his hands and with an embarrassed laugh hands it to Stella'**. Later in Scene 3, when the drunken Stanley regrets his actions towards Stella, he says, **'I want water'** and is subsequently put under the shower by his fellow poker players. His mood changes as he too is cleansed, emerging in his **'clinging wet polka dot drawers'**, ready to win back Stella.

In Scene 9, the symbolism of washing returns with Mitch's devastating line, **'You're not clean enough to bring in the house with my mother.'** Blanche, however, fights water with fire and ends the scene calling, **'Fire! Fire! Fire!'**

Light and shadows

In Williams's first description of Blanche he writes, *'Her delicate beauty must avoid a strong light' (Scene 1)*. Blanche's problematic relationship with light can be aligned to her aversion to realism. The most potent symbol of light in the play is the naked light bulb in the Kowalski apartment, which Blanche asks Mitch to cover with an *'adorable little coloured paper lantern'* at the beginning of their courtship *(Scene 3)*. In Scene 6, when they return from their date, she asks him to keep the lights off, instead lighting candle stubs. When their relationship is soured by Stanley, Mitch *'tears the paper lantern off the light-bulb'* and, despite her desperate pleading turns on the light, examining Blanche under its harsh glare *(Scene 9)*. The last poignant use of the lantern is in the final scene when Stanley *'seizes the paper lantern, tearing it off the light-bulb' (Scene 11)*. Blanche's identification with the torn paper lantern is confirmed by the stage direction, *'She cries out as if the lantern was herself' (Scene 11)*.

Shadows also appear in the stage directions, suggesting Blanche's fears and past. These *'lurid reflections'* are *'grotesque and menacing'*, highlighting Blanche's impending mental collapse *(Scene 10)*. They move *'sinuously as flames'*, foreshadowing Stanley's attack on her. They reappear in Scene 11, when she rushes past Stanley. It is only the soothing words of the Doctor which cause the shadows and noises to *'die out'*.

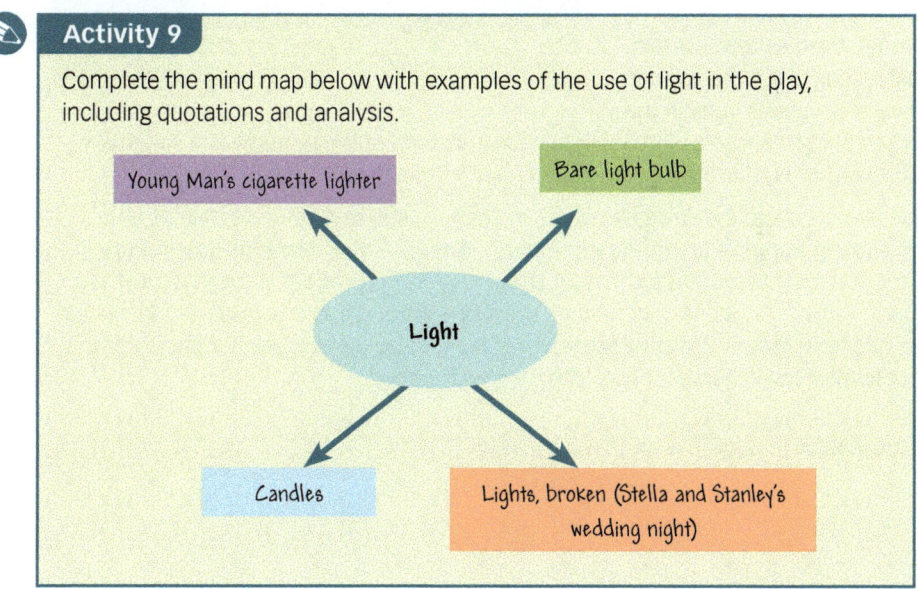

Activity 9

Complete the mind map below with examples of the use of light in the play, including quotations and analysis.

Young Man's cigarette lighter

Bare light bulb

Light

Candles

Lights, broken (Stella and Stanley's wedding night)

The streetcar

Williams had toyed with other titles for the play, including *The Moth* and *The Poker Night*, but ultimately settled on one that combines the concrete and tangible 'streetcar' with the abstract and emotional, 'desire'. The image was based on his personal experience in New Orleans. In 1946 Williams was living on St Peter Street in New Orleans. Nearby, he could see the local streetcars, including ones named 'Desire' and 'Cemeteries'. He noted that 'their indiscourageable progress up and down Royal Street struck me as having some symbolic bearing of a broad nature on the life in the Vieux Carre – and everywhere else, for that matter'.

Streetcars in 1940s' New Orleans

In the opening of the play, Blanche explains her confusing journey on the streetcars 'Desire' and 'Cemeteries', establishing for the audience the themes of love and death, reinforced by her final destination, Elysian Fields, which is an ancient Greek mythological land of the dead for heroic figures. This journey reflects both what has occurred before the play and her journey through the play towards her final resting place, the asylum. There is a hideous irony in the asylum being Blanche's ultimate destination, instead of the promise and sanctuary suggested by Elysian Fields at the end of her first journey.

Blanche returns to the streetcar when, in Scene 4, she says to Stella, **'What you are talking about is brutal desire – just – Desire! – the name of that rattle-trap streetcar that bangs through the Quarter, up one old narrow street and down another...'**. Stella understands the <mark>sub-text</mark> of her example, asking Blanche if she has **'ever ridden on that streetcar?'** Blanche acknowledges her past with the double meaning in her response, **'It brought me here.'**

> **sub-text** an underlying or unspoken meaning

Card game

The heading given to the third scene, 'The Poker Night' was also a draft title for the whole play, suggesting its importance to Williams's concept. Poker is a game of skill and luck, which involves holding your nerve and outwitting those around you. In Scene 3, Stanley is shown losing at cards and subsequently loses his temper as well, but by the final scene he is winning. He explains his philosophy: **'To hold front position in this rat-race you've got to believe you are lucky'** *(Scene 11)*. This contrasts with the fatally unlucky Blanche, whom he has beaten.

In both of the poker games (Scene 3 and Scene 11), the game is presented as a masculine activity which the women must skirt around. In Scene 11, Eunice remarks on the contrast between what the women are doing, readying for Blanche's departure, and the men's absorption in their game: **'I always did say that men are callous things with no feelings, but this does beat anything'** *(Scene 11)*. The poker game, with its emphasis on money and winning, is something from which the women are actively excluded.

The two poker scenes serve to trace Stanley's dominance over Blanche, as he has played his hand more astutely than she has. The humiliation of Blanche's exit is highlighted by the poker players' presence, indicating that life will go on much as it had before once she leaves. The final line, **'This game is seven-card stud'**, with its unmistakably masculine final word 'stud' (which can also mean a prized male animal kept for breeding), emphasizes the victory of the harsh 'rat-race' world over the delicate Blanche.

Activity 10

Choose one of the following symbols: washing, light and shadows, streetcars, card game, and create a spider diagram to analyse it.

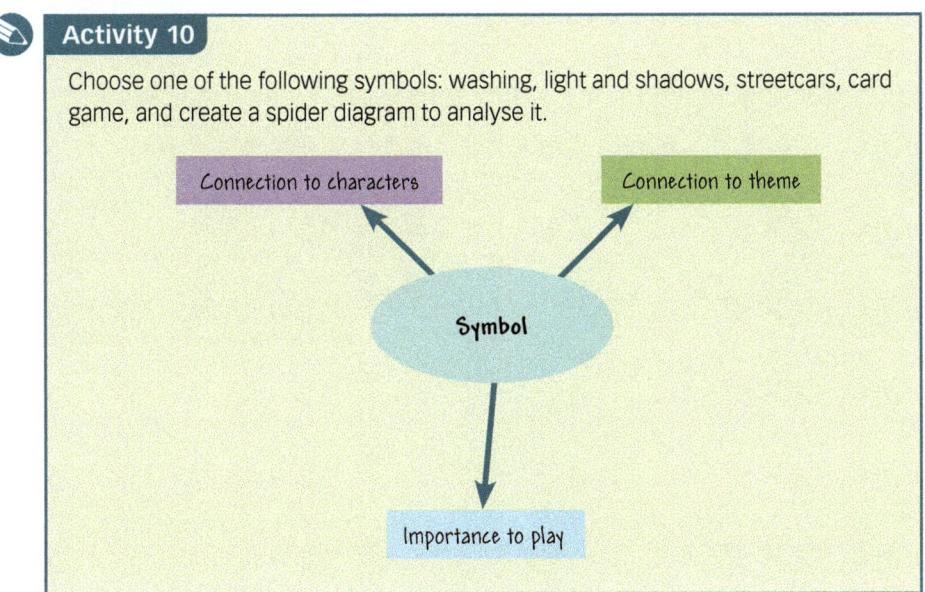

Irony

When Stanley replies 'Well, isn't that just dandy!' upon being told by Stella she's going out for dinner, he is being sarcastic *(Scene 2)*. This is a form of **irony** which he uses throughout the play. This sarcasm hits a more ominous note in Scene 10 when he says about Blanche's tiara: 'Gosh. I thought it was Tiffany diamonds.' He continues to lull her into a false sense of pleasant comradery: 'You having an oil-millionaire and me having a baby' *(Scene 10)*. However, the audience is aware of the irony and this increases the tension when he breaks the pretence by declaring, 'As a matter of fact there wasn't no wire at all' *(Scene 10)*.

An example of **dramatic irony** occurs at the end of Scene 4 when the audience is aware that Stanley can hear Blanche's complaints about him ('*He stands unseen by the women*'). The audience therefore understand that his behaviour in subsequent scenes is fuelled by what he has overheard. A more light-hearted example of dramatic irony occurs in Scene 6 when Blanche speaks in French to Mitch. Audiences with some knowledge of French may recognize the seductive question, '*Voulez-vous couchez avec moi ce soir?*', as a sexual overture, but Mitch is entirely unaware of what she has said to him and believes her to be prim and proper. Blanche is ironically presented as both sexually knowing and innocent.

> **dramatic irony** irony used to make the audience aware of something unknown to the characters
>
> **irony** words that express the opposite of what is meant; the difference between what may be expected and what actually occurs

The jewels in Blanche's tiara are cheap rhinestones, rather than expensive diamonds, which mirror her attempts to portray her life in a more glamorous light

Activity 11

Read the following student's paragraph about the use of irony in the play and then add an additional paragraph of your own.

> Williams's use of irony increases the tension in the play, particularly in the interplay between Stanley and Blanche. Stanley frequently punctures Blanche's affectations with sarcasm, such as his response to Blanche's request that he 'possess' his 'soul in patience!' with 'It's not my soul I'm worried about!' *(Scene 7)*. When he presents Blanche with her birthday present, the audience knows before Blanche that it is a one-way ticket back to Laurel, so not a gift at all. Although Blanche is aware that she is unwelcome by Stanley, she is unaware of the lengths to which he has gone to expose her past. However the audience knows, from the end of Scene 4 after he has overheard her speech to Stella and he 'grins through the curtains at Blanche', that he will never forgive her. This makes her attempts to be entertaining at her birthday supper and to win back Mitch all the more pathetic.

Writing about language

Upgrade

Analysis of language is essential to writing well about the play. When checking over your work, ensure that you have:

- used correct literary terminology like 'symbolism' and 'allusion'
- explained the effect of the literary techniques, such as providing insight into the characters, creating tension, enhancing themes
- provided short, well-selected quotations to support your points
- considered what the characters' dialogue, including diction and punctuation, reveal about them
- reflected upon how Williams's writing style reinforces the atmosphere and themes of his play.

Williams's play is rich with **themes**, which he explores through the play's plot, characterization, setting and dialogue. Key themes include social class, madness, love and death.

> **themes** key ideas or recurring subjects which appear in a work of literature

Social class

Throughout the play, Williams pointedly stakes out the differences between the DuBois and Kowalski families. Blanche represents the dying southern aristocracy while Stanley is an example of the emerging immigrant working class. The differences in their social class are shown though their dialogue, their education, their attitudes towards money and their friendships. Stella has made a transition from her genteel upbringing to her working-class married life, claiming her new modest surroundings are **'not that bad at all!'** *(Scene 1)*. Blanche tries to impose her etiquette on the Kowalski household, e.g. expecting that men will rise when a woman enters the room unless told specifically not to, but she is quickly disabused by the brusque Stanley: **'Nobody's going to get up, so don't be worried'** *(Scene 3)*.

At times, Stella begins to see her life from Blanche's perspective, e.g. laughing at her neighbours: **'You ought to see their wives'** *(Scene 3)*. When Stella tries to explain Blanche's expectations – **'you've got to realize that Blanche and I grew up under very different circumstances than you did'** *(Scene 7)* – Stanley becomes enraged, believing that she thinks they are better than him. In Scene 8, Stanley remembers when Stella showed him **'a snapshot of the place with the columns'** and takes particular pride in having **'pulled'** her **'down off them columns'** *(Scene 8)*.

Belle Reve is symbolic of the land-owning southern social class and its loss is a blow. It has left Blanche poor and homeless with nothing to 'protect' her, while Stanley had hoped to inherit it in accordance with the **'Napoleonic code'**. Instead of an inheritance, their future now rests entirely on Stanley's **'drive'**. Blanche acknowledges this when she says, **'he's what we need to mix with our blood'** *(Scene 2)*. A surrender to her new position in the world is reflected in Blanche's pursuit of Mitch, an ordinary working-class man with no particular prospects, simply because he will be able to provide a home for her.

Belle Reve could have been a typical 'Deep South' plantation house, like this one

Activity 1

Use a table like the one below to compare how Williams presents the difference in social class between Blanche and Stanley.

	Stanley	Blanche
Etiquette		
Dialogue		
Occupation		
Interests		

Masculinity and femininity

In Scene 3, the drawn portières (curtains) in the Kowalski apartment create a metaphoric battle line between the masculine and the feminine. On one side, the men are drinking and playing cards, on the other the women undress and listen to the radio. Blanche draws attention to the attractions of the feminine side when she undresses and either consciously or unconsciously stands in the light. Mitch, who the men have treated as a 'mama's boy' (**'we'll fix you a sugar-tit'**) *(Scene 3)* is drawn to the women's side of the room, much to Stanley's annoyance.

In various ways, Williams clearly differentiates between the women's world and the men's. Stella accepts that Stanley's interest in bowling and poker is **'his pleasure'**, contrasting with hers in **'movies and bridge'** *(Scene 4)*. However, the divisions go beyond their hobbies and extend into their expected societal roles. Stanley's throwing of the red-stained butcher's package in Scene 1 is symbolic of his role as the 'hunter-gatherer': it demonstrates that he will provide for his family. Stella explains to Blanche that **'Stanley doesn't give me a regular allowance, he likes to pay bills himself'**, though in an act of contrition for the previous night he has given her ten dollars *(Scene 4)*. It is Stella's role to prepare the meals, which explains Stanley's annoyance at being left a **'cold plate on ice'** instead of a hot meal in Scene 2. Stella is further fulfilling her feminine role by becoming a mother and the progress of her pregnancy is one of the determiners of the play's timescale.

Stanley has clear ideas on what it is to be a man and asserts that he is **'the king around here'** *(Scene 8)*. Within his friendship group, he is the 'alpha male', whose moods dominate their poker games. Mitch, on the other hand, provides more complex gender signals. He appears to be like a bear, typically a masculine image, but Blanche also describes him has having a **'sensitive look'** *(Scene 3)*. Another unconventional male figure is presented in Blanche's account of her dead husband, who she identifies as possessing **'a nervousness, a softness and tenderness which wasn't like a man's, although he wasn't the least bit effeminate-looking – still – that thing was there'** *(Scene 6)*. Several of the play's characters do not easily fall into the rigidly prescribed gender roles.

Activity 2

Write two paragraphs expressing your agreement or disagreement with the following statement: Williams punishes those who do not conform to traditional mid-20ᵗʰ-century gender roles.

Love, sex and marriage

More explicitly than was usual for a play in the 1940s, *A Streetcar Named Desire* deals with sex. From the 'Desire' in the title to the final image in Scene 11 when Stanley's **'fingers find the opening'** of Stella's blouse, sex permeates the play. Stella refers to its dominance when she says, **'But there are things that happen between a man and a woman in the dark – that sort of make everything else seem – unimportant'** *(Scene 4)*. For Stella, her lust has led to love and marriage with Stanley. Blanche acknowledges that it is the streetcar *Desire* which **'brought me here'** *(Scene 4)*, referring not only to the literal streetcar but to the expressions of desire in Laurel with younger men, which led to her losing her job and finding herself homeless. She is a fugitive from the small-town expectations of a spinster school teacher. However, the New Orleans she arrives in is one of sexual permissiveness: a clip joint on the corner, drunken propositions and the temptations of **'long rainy afternoons'** *(Scene 5)*.

Blanche, in her youth, has known love. Stella describes Blanche's feelings towards Allan Grey powerfully: she **'didn't just love him but worshipped the ground he walked on! Adored him and thought him almost too fine to be human'** *(Scene 7)*. After her disastrous marriage and in order to escape the reminders of 'Death' which surrounded her, she sought out the company of young men: **'But sometimes I slipped outside to answer their calls'** *(Scene 9)*. She was **'hunting for some protection'** even if it meant finding it in **'unlikely places – even, at last, in a seventeen-year old boy'** *(Scene 9)*.

In New Orleans, Blanche uses her sexual appeal in a more calculated way, hoping to ensnare Mitch as a husband: **'I want to *deceive* him enough to make him – want me'** *(Scene 5)*. Although she hopes he will desire her, her feelings towards him are more practical: **'I want to *rest*! [...] If it happens! I can leave here and not be anyone's problem'** *(Scene 5)*. Mitch's proposal to her is not one full of passion or sexual desire, but a gentle recognition of their mutual need: **'You need somebody. And I need somebody, too'** *(Scene 6)*. Even after Mitch's cruel treatment of her in Scene 9, Blanche's desperate willingness to trade sex for marriage is apparent in her final plea, **'Then marry me, Mitch!'** When Mitch dismisses her as not being **'clean'** and therefore unsuitable for marriage, the relationship and Blanche's hope of finding a husband ends.

Activity 3

Read the following quotations and then choose a selection of them for a paragraph explaining the attitudes towards sex and marriage presented in the play.

- **Yes, I had many intimacies with strangers.** *(Blanche, Scene 9)*

- **That pitch about your ideals being so old-fashioned and all the malarkey that you've dished out all summer.** *(Mitch, Scene 9)*

- **Well, he's not going to marry her. Maybe he** *was*, **but he's not going to jump in a tank with a school of sharks – now!** *(Stanley, Scene 7)*

- **People don't see you –** *men* **don't – don't even admit your existence unless they are making love to you.** *(Blanche, Scene 5)*

- **He hasn't gotten a thing but a good-night kiss, that's all I have given him, Stella. I want his respect.** *(Blanche, Scene 5)*

- **Just give me a slap whenever I step out of bounds.** *(Mitch, Scene 6)*

- **I loved someone, too, and the person I loved I lost.** *(Blanche, Scene 6)*

- **By coming suddenly into a room that I thought was empty – which wasn't empty, but had two people in it...** *(Blanche, Scene 6)*

Activity 4

a) Read the excerpt below discussing the relationship between men and women.

> There the two sisters argue about Stanley. His sexual attractiveness is not questioned, but his worthiness as a marriage partner is. The conflict here is between Blanche's romantic, essentially asexual view of marriage, which may have led her to marry a homosexual but is hardly consonant with her subsequent promiscuity, and Stella's understanding that marriage is one avenue for sexual fulfillment, a channel for her healthy sexual appetite. Ostensibly Stella and conventional heterosexual marriage win, but only through Stella's denying the truth about Stanley's rape of Blanche. For all Stanley's macho posturing, it is Stella's denial that sends Blanche to the asylum, not Stanley's rape.
>
> (John M. Clum, 'The sacrificial stud and the fugitive female in *Suddenly Last Summer*, *Orpheus Descending* and *Sweet Bird of Youth*', *The Cambridge Companion to Tennessee Williams*)

b) To what extent do you agree that it is Stella's denial of the rape, rather than the rape itself, that sends Blanche to the asylum?

Reality versus illusion

> **Key quotation**
>
> **I'll tell you what I want. Magic! [*Mitch laughs*.] Yes, yes, magic! I try to give that to people. I misrepresent things to them. I don't tell the truth. I tell what *ought* to be truth. And if that is sinful, then let me be damned for it! – *Don't turn the light on!***
> (Blanche, Scene 9)

Blanche's life is a struggle between the **'magic'** she desires and the harsh realities that assault her. It is no accident that when she retreats to the bathroom in Scene 7, she sings a song in praise of pretence and imagination: **'It's a Barnum and Bailey world, Just as phoney as it can be – But it wouldn't be make-believe If you believed in me.'** Williams depicts Blanche's struggle to entertain and put on a performance, while facing the derision of characters like Stanley. She employs a number of methods to keep reality at bay. She dresses up, flirts, sings, adjusts the lighting, dances and tells jokes. The distance between reality and fantasy is clear in the opening of Scene 6. Mitch and Blanche return from what should have been a light-hearted date to an amusement park, but are exhausted and depressed. Mitch remarks on his failure to provide entertainment and Blanche notes the gap between her efforts and the **'dismal mess'** of the evening.

Once inside the apartment, Blanche tries to create a magical atmosphere by pretending they are in **'a little artists' café on the Left Bank in Paris'** *(Scene 6)*. She lights candles, pours drinks and speaks in French, including the daring invitation to sleep with her, **'Voulez-vous couchez avec moi ce soir?'**, uttered only because she knows Mitch does not speak French. She is risking discovery of her true nature, exclaiming, **'I mean it's a damned good thing'** that Mitch doesn't understand French and later rolling her eyes **'knowing he cannot see her face'** when she is proclaiming her **'old-fashioned ideals'** *(Scene 6)*. Ironically, it is not Blanche's artifice which wins Mitch, but her honest admission of loneliness and her description of the sad end to her marriage.

Blanche, played here by Vivien Leigh in the 1951 film, lies about her relationship with drink

Blanche admits that she lies. In Scene 5, when composing her letter to Shep Huntleigh, she laughs at herself for being **'such a liar'**. The audience is confronted with the gap between her description of her visit to her sister – **'a continued round of entertainments, teas, cocktails, and luncheons'** – and the reality of the poker games, fighting neighbours and the Four Deuces nightclub. Blanche uses alcohol to dull the harsh reality which surrounds her, but is also untruthful about her use of alcohol, claiming to Stanley in Scene 1 that she only rarely touches it.

Another source of magic and unreality is represented by Belle Reve. Stella has shown Stanley a photograph of it and the audience glimpses what their upbringing there was like through Blanche's wardrobe and social expectations. However Belle Reve means 'beautiful dream' and its loss is also the loss of the family's dreams. Williams's mother Edwina similarly idealized their life in Mississippi and mourned its loss when they moved, yet retained the affectations of a southern belle.

On the other hand, Stanley represents brutal reality. He notes that **'Some men are took in by this Hollywood glamour stuff and some men are not'**, firmly aligning himself with the second group *(Scene 2)*. When Blanche attempts to evade and flirt, he shouts **'Now let's cut the re-bop'** *(Scene 2)*. Doubting Blanche's honesty, he asks a colleague to contact a merchant in Laurel to discover Blanche's past. He is brutal in his search for the truth and determined to extricate Blanche from his household. In Scene 11, he says to her, **'You left nothing here but spilt talcum and old empty perfume bottles'**, both signs of her attempts at glamour, and then tears down her paper lantern, the last remnant of her time at the apartment.

At the end of the play, however, it is Blanche who has told the truth about Stanley's actions, while Stanley has lied to Stella. Stella chooses to believe him because otherwise she couldn't **'go on living with Stanley'** *(Scene 11)*. Eunice and Stella, in turn, lie to Blanche, convincing her that she is going on a vacation. At the end of the play, Blanche seems uncertain what is reality and what is fantasy, but the final line in Scene 11 – **'This game is seven-card stud'** – indicates a return to reality for the inhabitants of Elysian Fields.

Activity 5

Copy and complete the spider diagram below with your observations about truth and **'magic'** in the play.

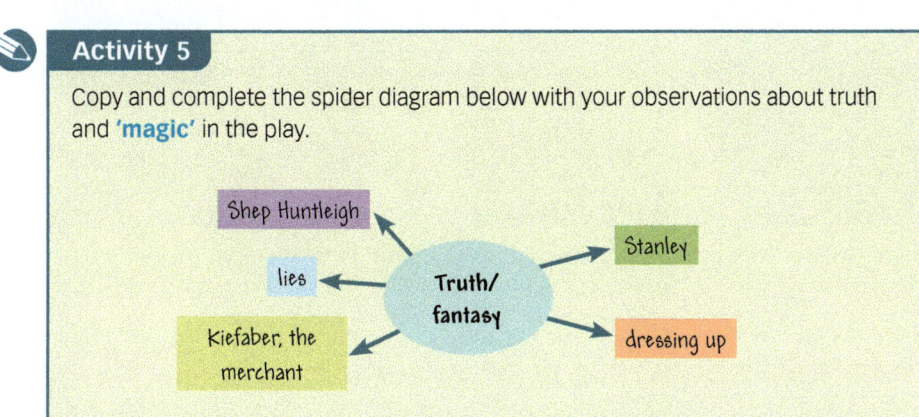

Madness

The subject of madness runs through Williams's life and work. As well as his own struggles with alcoholism and mental health, his sister Rose suffered from mental illness. She was prone to periods of hysteria and was said at times to be violent. Her family eventually decided to have her undergo a lobotomy, hoping that it would destroy 'the chain of memory […] so that one lives without being tortured by fantasies' (Ronald Hayman, *Tennessee Williams: Everyone Else is an Audience*. Yale University Press, New Haven, 1993, page 48). When Williams learned of the lobotomy, he was said to have felt guilty. He kept a photograph of Rose over his writing desk and she is believed to have influenced a number of his characters including Laura in *The Glass Menagerie* and Blanche.

One way that Williams depicts Blanche's mental state is through the use of sound and music. In the first scene, Blanche's nervous disposition is characterized through her reactions to sounds such as when a cat screeches she *'catches her breath with a startled gesture'* and needs to calm herself with a drink. At the end of the scene *'The music of the polka rises up'*, which the audience later connects with the death of Blanche's husband, and leads to her line, *'the boy died'*.

Gillian Anderson shows Blanche's nervous disposition in the 2014 Young Vic production

Throughout the play, the music of Elysian Fields, the *'blue piano'*, competes with the Varsouviana polka, as Blanche's present and past intermingle. In Scene 6, Blanche tells Mitch about the death of her husband. Williams heightens this effect through the use of sound effects. First a locomotive is heard, causing an extreme reaction in Blanche, when she covers her ears and *'crouches over'*. Then the polka music underscores her description of dancing at the Moon Lake Casino. The music increases at the end of her story, but *'fades out'* when Mitch kisses her, as if absolving her from her past. However, by Scene 9, her demons have reappeared and she is drinking to escape the music and *'the sense of disaster closing in on her'* (Scene 9). She has lost control of her memories and at one point has to wait for the sound of a *'distant revolver shot'* before being able to continue speaking to Mitch (Scene 9). By Scene 10, Blanche is fully hallucinating *'spectral admirers'*, unaware of the pathetic spectacle she makes in her *'soiled and crumpled'* fancy clothes.

However, even when seemingly at her weakest, Blanche has moments of lucidity and insight. In Scene 9, she still tries to convince Mitch to marry her, possibly hoping that her truth-telling, which was so effective in Scene 6, will work again. She is also able to fight off his sexual advances. In Scene 10, she correctly reads Stanley's intentions and attempts to escape him. In Scene 11, she is confused, but aware enough to know that she wants to avoid the poker-playing men and she quickly recognizes that the Doctor is a stranger to her. Her final destination is a mental institution, where there are hints of the possible treatments when the Matron refers to trimming her fingernails, presumably to avoid her scratching herself or anyone else if violent, and indicates that they have a straitjacket to hand if necessary to restrain her.

Activity 6

Williams suggests several possible sources of Blanche's mental instability. Some possibilities are:

- grief at the death of her husband
- a personal weakness, first shown in her **'flighty'** nature
- the gulf between her dreams and her reality
- her sensitive, imaginative nature
- her vulnerability at the hands of cruel people
- her dependency on alcohol.

Think about these different ideas and decide which reason or reasons seem most likely to you. Number the list in order of importance and add evidence from the play next to each bullet point.

Tips for assessment

When writing about a theme, try to connect the different times and ways it is explored by the playwright. A theme is a big idea that runs throughout a play, not something that happens just once in isolation.

Death

Although the more famous streetcar in the play leads to Desire, the other's destination is Cemeteries. Death, personified in Scene 1 as the Grim Reaper, shadows the play. In her first dialogue with Stella, Blanche refers to the high-school superintendent Mr Graves, whose actions led to her leave of absence. In her explanation of the loss of Belle Reve she focuses on the family deaths, the harsh reality of which fell on her, while Stella was in New Orleans with Stanley.

Activity 8

a) Closely read Blanche's speech in Scene 1, which begins, **'I, I, *I* took the blows in my face and my body!'** and ends with **'In bed with your – Polak!'** Highlight every mention of death.

b) Next analyse these key phrases:

- **The long parade to the graveyard!**
- **But had to be burned like rubbish!**
- **And funerals are pretty compared to deaths.**
- **Death is expensive, Miss Stella!**
- **Why, the Grim Reaper had put up his tent on our doorstep!**

c) Lastly, write a paragraph explaining your impression of this speech and the effect it might have on the audience.

In Scene 3, Mitch and Blanche bond over a quotation from the poem 'How Do I Love Thee?' by Elizabeth Barrett Browning: '**… and if God choose,/I shall but love thee better after death.**'

Death also follows Mitch, with his sad attachment to the girl who is 'dead now' (Scene 3) and his fear of the death of his ill mother. He responds sensitively to the story of Blanche's husband's death.

> **Key quotation**
>
> **Blanche:** I loved someone, too, and the person I loved I lost.
>
> **Mitch:** Dead? [*She crosses to the window and sits on the sill, looking out. She pours herself another drink.*] A man? (Scene 6)

His response leads to Blanche's willingness to reveal her vulnerability and guilt.

Although the play does not end with Blanche's death, but instead her exile to an asylum, images of death haunt her. She tries to escape these memories but they are represented on stage in an expressionistic way, through the use of shadows, music and the mysterious Mexican vendor, selling flowers for the dead.

In contrast to the death imagery, Stella's life represents both a symbolic rebirth, as she settles into a life apparently unscathed by the problems in Laurel, and actual birth, as she is revealed to be pregnant in Scene 2. Blanche's destruction coincides with the introduction of a new life in the Kowalski household.

Activity 9

In Scene 11, Blanche presents an idealized version of her own death, which she imagines will be very different from that of her family in Belle Reve. Read the speech, starting with, **'I can smell the sea air'** and ending with **'my first lover's eyes** (Scene 11). Then answer the following questions.

a) What do you think the significance of an **'unwashed grape'** might be?

b) What are the attractions of dying at sea for Blanche?

c) What is the significance of the last line of the speech?

Tips for assessment

If you are asked to write about a theme from the play, you will be expected to understand how that theme has been presented by the playwright in all elements of the play. This includes what the characters say, what the characters do, how the stage directions suggest a theme, and how the story of the whole play moves and develops because of the theme.

Shame and humiliation

In Scene 10, Stanley tells a story about his cousin. At first, it appears that it is going to be a joke about someone who is a 'human-bottle opener' but, after the cousin breaks off his front teeth, it turns sour – 'he was so ashamed of himself he used t' sneak out of the house when company came' (Scene 10) – and it becomes a cautionary tale. The story can simply be interpreted as Stanley explaining why he is looking for a bottle-opener, but it seems to have a more ominous message about public shame. His cousin was performing 'his only accomplishment' in a very public place, a wedding party, and thereafter, after losing his front teeth, felt shame and shunned the company of others. Stanley views his cousin with no sympathy, as if he deserved his sad fate for showing off and outliving his usefulness. Stanley also endeavours to humiliate Blanche and to send her away in shame.

There are a number of examples of humiliation for Blanche. Allan Grey's death happens in a public place. After an exchange of words on a dance floor, he shoots himself nearby: 'I ran out – all did – all ran and gathered about the terrible thing at the edge of the lake! I couldn't get near for crowding' (Scene 6). His death, as well as her reaction, is witnessed by all. Later, when her actions in Laurel have become notorious, she is fired from her job as a teacher. Stanley claims he would have liked to have witnessed her humiliation: 'Boy, oh, boy, I'd like to have been in that office when Dame Blanche was called on the carpet' (Scene 7). She suffers further humiliation when her modest birthday supper is marred by Mitch's very visible absence, represented by the empty chair at the table – 'There is a fourth place at the table which is left vacant' (Scene 8) – a reminder that her modest dream of marrying Mitch is to be thwarted. In Scene 11, her agonizing departure to the asylum, her final humiliation, is witnessed by the poker players and neighbours.

Blanche tries to reinterpret events to soften the shame that she feels. When crowds of suitors no longer pursue her, she invents 'spectral admirers' (Scene 10). Shep Huntleigh becomes the image of a rich saviour, who in her imagination is only ever a telephone call, telegram or doorbell ring away. Devastated by Mitch's rejection, she imagines a noble conversation in which she has uttered the unlikely lines, 'We have to be realistic about such things. So farewell, my friend! And let there be no hard feelings...' (Scene 10). Even with the arrival of the Doctor, Blanche rallies her spirits enough to imagine a world in which, instead of shame, humiliation and cruelty, she can find kindness.

The public absolving of sins is a common feature of tragedies. The ancient Greek tragedy *Oedipus Rex* by Sophocles ends with the tragic hero Oedipus blinding himself in an effort to 'unsee' his unwitting past crimes of killing his father and marrying his own mother. He publicly reveals his shame, observed by Creon, the ruler of Thebes, and the Chorus. Creon makes efforts to hide Oedipus from onlookers:

> The unclean must not remain in the eye of day;
> Nor earth nor air nor water may receive it.
> Take him within; piety at least demands
> That none but kinsmen should hear and see such suffering.
>
> (Sophocles, *Oedipus Rex*)

Oedipus is eventually escorted off to his lengthy exile, while order is restored in the city of Thebes.

 Activity 10

With a partner, discuss the similarities and differences between the handling of shame in the endings of *Oedipus Rex* and *A Streetcar Named Desire*.

Writing about themes

To revise themes, try the following activities.

- Make a table recording the key points of development of each theme.
- Consider how context, e.g. contemporary attitudes towards gender roles or social class, might influence your understanding of the themes.
- Memorize key quotations that provide examples of themes.
- Analyse the language used to make a theme vivid, e.g. how death is depicted.
- Question what Williams's attitude towards the theme might be and what he is trying to convey to the audience through its exploration.
- Connect your understanding of themes with your insight into Williams's use of symbolism, e.g. how 'light' can be used symbolically to demonstrate the theme of realism versus illusion, or how the expressionistic use of music can illuminate the themes of madness or death.

When writing about plays, it is important to consider the different ways the text has been interpreted in production. Fortunately for students, *A Streetcar Named Desire* is an extremely popular play, which has been re-imagined over the decades on stage and in film, providing a wealth of material for analysis.

First performance

A Streetcar Named Desire had its first Broadway performance on 3 December 1947 and was an immediate triumph, going on to win the Pulitzer Prize and the New York Drama Critics' Circle award. However, the success of the play owed a debt not only to the brilliance of Williams's script, but also to the directing, acting and design of the production. As a prominent critic of the time, Brooks Atkinson said about Williams, he 'is no literal dramatist and writes in none of the conventional forms, he presents the theatre with many problems' (reported in *New York Times*, December 1947). Below are some of the key contributions of Williams's collaborators.

Directing

Elia Kazan was one of the most sought-after directors of his time and Williams acknowledged his skill as the 'one-man theatre that brought *Streetcar* before the widest possible audience' (Williams talking about Kazan in 'Tenessee Tells All'). Kazan had a background in highly realistic and political theatre, and was known for helping actors to discover the psychological motivations and actions of their characters. He also worked with Williams on the script, encouraging cuts and other changes. Some critics felt that although Kazan said he agreed with Williams that Blanche was the protagonist of the play, he seemed to be more attracted to Stanley as a character, leading at times to an imbalance, with Blanche's position as sensitive, misunderstood outsider being lost.

Acting

A Streetcar Named Desire made the previously little known 25-year-old Marlon Brando a star. Williams wrote about his casting: 'It humanizes the character of Stanley in that it becomes the brutality or callousness of youth rather than a vicious older man. I don't want to focus guilt or blame on any one character but to have it a tragedy of misunderstanding and insensitivity to others' (letter to Audrey Wood, 1947). Jessica Tandy, a 38-year-old English actress with a classical background, was chosen to play Blanche and received enthusiastic reviews, citing her ability to 'understand such an elusive part so thoroughly' and convey it 'with so many shades and impulses that are accurate, revealing and true' (Brooks Atkinson reported in *New York Times*, December 1947). However, other critics felt that she was not entirely believable or sympathetic in the role, e.g. finding it impossible to believe that she had a sordid past.

Design

The designer Jo Mielziner accepted the challenge of creating a set which incorporated both the realism and expressionism dictated by Williams's script, as well as establishing both the exterior and interior locations. He created the walls of the Kowalski flat with **scrims**, which could become transparent, and furnished it with realistic worn props and furnishings. Writing about his design, Mielziner said:

Rehearsals on the Mielziner set on tour at the Aldwych Theatre, London, in 1949

 When I designed *Streetcar*, I used translucent walls that could be made to appear by the skilled use of light and focus the attention of the audience on only one section of the stage at a given moment. The magic of light opened up a fluid and poetic world of storytelling – selective light that revealed or concealed, advanced a set or made it recede.'

(Jo Mielziner, *Designing for the Theatre: A Memoir and a Portfolio*)

scrims gauze screens which can be opaque or transparent depending on how they are lit

Tips for assessment

Demonstrating your knowledge of different productions allows you to show your understanding of the many ways the play can be interpreted. You may wish to contrast different interpretations and explain which most closely aligns with your own view.

 Activity 1

Identify at least three moments in which you believe lighting is important and consider what they could convey to the audience about the play and its themes.

Film

Elia Kazan, who directed the original Broadway production, also directed the 1951 film of the play. He replaced Jessica Tandy with Vivien Leigh, a much better known film actress who had played the role of Blanche in the first London production, but kept Marlon Brando, Kim Hunter and Karl Malden in their roles.

While retaining much of the original production, Kazan and Williams were required to make a number of changes in the script in order to satisfy the censors of the day. Two major changes included removing suggestions that Blanche's husband was homosexual and downplaying Blanche's attraction to younger men. Although it was a point of contention, the rape scene largely remained as written, with additional devices such as filming some of the scene in the reflection of a mirror and then smashing the mirror to symbolically indicate the shattering of Blanche. At the end of the movie, instead of the reconciliation of the play, Stella announces she will never trust her husband again. She is shown running upstairs to Eunice's apartment, clutching her baby, while ignoring Stanley's cries of 'Stella!'.

In 1984, a television film starred Ann Margaret and Treat Williams. This colour film opened the film out to capture the New Orleans setting. Scene 10 is shot in a candlelit room, with Ann Margaret as a still beautiful and graceful Blanche. The rape is more graphically portrayed than in the earlier film with Stanley straddling the prone Blanche and ripping at her clothes as she screams. The film ends after Blanche is escorted from the room, with Stella and Stanley embracing and walking with their arms around each other, back to the poker players. The last shot of the film is of the car carrying Blanche disappearing down a long road to the sound of church bells.

In 1995, Jessica Lange and Alec Baldwin featured in a television movie which was a filmic record of their 1992 Broadway production. The production received mixed reviews but was praised for adhering more closely to the original script than the 1951 film. Lange was considered a resilient Blanche who does not shy away from her desire for younger men and is resolute in her desire to protect her sister, though some felt she missed the pathos and fragility of the character.

In 2013, Woody Allen directed Cate Blanchett, who a few years previously had played a well-received Blanche on stage, and Alec Baldwin, who had previously played Stanley, in the film *Blue Jasmine*. Although it does not directly use Williams's script, it was clearly inspired by it.

Activity 2

Complete a table like the one below to compare the 1951 and 1984 films.

	1951 film	1984 film
Lighting/colour/symbolism		
Depiction of rape scene		
Ending of film		

Revivals

Important 21st-century revivals include the Trevor Nunn production starring Glenn Close at the National Theatre (2002); Rachel Weisz in Rob Ashford's production at the Donmar Warehouse (2009); Cate Blanchett directed by Liv Ullman in the Sydney Theatre Company (2009); and Benedict Andrews' production starring Gillian Anderson, which premiered at the Young Vic Theatre in London (2014). All of these productions featured outstanding actresses, each of whom put her own stamp on the character of Blanche. These productions used primarily realistic sets, with some highlighting the period and New Orleans. There are some key differences between the productions:

- Unlike the other three revivals, Benedict Andrews's production was updated to the present day and set **in the round** with a modern, primarily white and grey set. The set slowly revolved throughout the play so every member of the audience had a slightly different view. The bathroom, which is often offstage, was visible to the audience, and Gillian Anderson and other actors changed costumes onstage. After the rape scene, Anderson, partially dressed, showered onstage.

- Rob Ashford's production externalized the figures, like her dead husband, who haunt Blanche by having them appear on stage at key moments. The set emphasized the New Orleans setting with ornamental balconies and a graceful curved staircase.

- The set of the Sydney Theatre Company's production was particularly cramped, with the bathroom a walled-off room within the main room, heightening the sense of claustrophobia, while giving little indication of the New Orleans setting.

- In contrast, the set for the National Theatre production was a towering tenement. The set periodically revolved to reveal or give prominence to one of four settings: the main room, the bedroom, the bathroom or outside. Extra characters, like a nun and a prostitute, as well as a jazz quintet, were added to create the New Orleans atmosphere of the outdoor scenes.

Rachel Weisz as Blanche, with Ruth Wilson as Stella, in the 2009 Donmar Warehouse production

in the round a theatre configuration where the audience is positioned all around the stage, rather than just in front of it

Activity 3

a) Read the description of these two performances of Blanche and then write a paragraph explaining which more closely coincides with your ideas of how Blanche should be played.

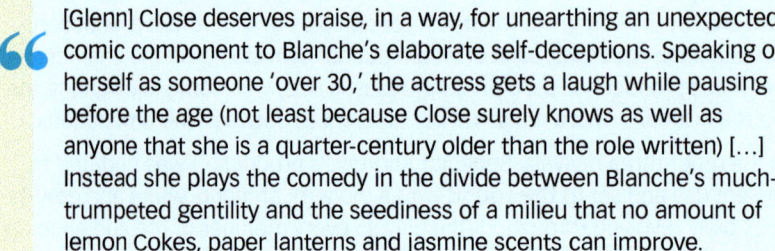

[Glenn] Close deserves praise, in a way, for unearthing an unexpectedly comic component to Blanche's elaborate self-deceptions. Speaking of herself as someone 'over 30,' the actress gets a laugh while pausing before the age (not least because Close surely knows as well as anyone that she is a quarter-century older than the role written) [...] Instead she plays the comedy in the divide between Blanche's much-trumpeted gentility and the seediness of a milieu that no amount of lemon Cokes, paper lanterns and jasmine scents can improve.

(Matt Wolf, *Variety*, 9 October 2002)

But what Weisz brings to the role is a quality of desperate solitude touched with grace. This is a woman who, whatever her shady past, values 'beauty of the mind and richness of the spirit and tenderness of the heart.' When Weisz utters these words, it is with such impassioned sincerity that you lament the waste of a noble, refined soul.

(Michael Billington, *The Guardian*, 29 July 2009)

b) Read the excerpts below from the National Theatre's costume list, detailing Blanche's (Glenn Close) and Stanley's (Iain Glen) first scene costumes:

Blanche: corselette, stockings, petticoat, chiffon frill-necked blouse, chiffon layered shirt, ivory jacket, pearl necklace, earrings, hat, gloves, handbag.

Stanley: Jeans, work boots, sweaty grey vest, leather jacket, white jersey boxer shorts.

c) Now complete the following sentence: From their initial costumes, the designer was hoping to convey...

d) Next, compare Glenn Close's costumes above with this description of Gillian Anderson's costume in the updated 2014 production:

Large sunglasses, a stylish pale oyster dress with matching jacket, a small gold shoulder bag, very high heels. She is pulling a wheelie suitcase, topped with a Louis Vuitton bag.

e) Then complete this following sentence: The designer has updated Blanche's costumes by...

Tips for assessment

When you are analysing a performance, remember to look beyond what you are seeing and ask yourself what this is *showing* you about the play or the character.

Alternative readings

A Streetcar Named Desire has been re-interpreted in ways which have challenged the gender, ethnic and genre choices of the original.

In 1991, a collaboration between members of two performance groups, Split Britches and Bloolips, resulted in a radical reworking of the play called *Belle Reprieve*. Challenging typical gender roles, a man dressed as a woman (Bette Bourne) played Blanche while a woman (Peggy Shaw) played Stanley. The production explored the performance nature of gender roles and sought to draw out and parody the assumptions and stereotypes of the original through musical hall songs, skits and dance.

In 2011, experimental American playwright and director Lee Breuer led a controversial production *Un Tramway Nommé Désir* at the Comédie Française. Performed in French, this production had many influences, especially traditional Japanese theatre. Against a backdrop of Japanese screens, Blanche was costumed in a kimono, while stagehands appeared to deliver props or change scenes. In one scene, Stanley smears white shaving cream on his face to approximate a Japanese kabuki mask. To re-create aspects of the New Orleans atmosphere, a jazz trio and singers performed. The lack of naturalism was emphasized in Scene 3, when a drunken Stanley, wearing only a towel, shouted for Stella. She descended down a flywire in order to carry him back to the upper levels. Breuer wished to break from the conventions of the Kazan film and to explore the rules of the old South through the formal conventions of Japanese theatre, while adding his own avant-garde take on the material.

In 2012, Emily Mann directed a production which highlighted the multi-racial aspect of New Orleans by casting African-American actors Nicole Ari Parker and Blair Underwood as Blanche and Stanley, and Daphne Rubin-Vega, a Panamanian-American actress, as Stella. The production introduced the setting with a parade of the diverse inhabitants of the French quarter. Parker's interpretation was of a robust, canny Blanche eventually destroyed by the cruelty of Underwood's powerful Stanley.

In contrast, director Sean Holmes produced a stripped-back version on a simple minimalistic white set in 2014. The cast did not use American accents, but instead spoke in their natural English accents (or Estonian accent for one actor) and there was no attempt to capture the world of New Orleans. Blanche was played by Nadia Albina, who is missing the lower half of one arm. Casting a performer with a visible disability encouraged audiences to re-examine their ideas about independence and beauty.

Blanche, played by Nadia Albina in the 2014 Lyric Hammersmith production

Activity 4

Read the excerpt from the interview by Lyn Gardner in *The Guardian* with Nadia Albina and then answer the questions below.

 Albina says that, as a disabled woman, she is used to feeling 'isolated, not belonging, an alien in your surroundings' and all those feelings are heartbreakingly apparent in her Blanche, a woman who also feels like an alien in her surroundings.

(Lyn Gardner, 'My disability helped me understand Blanche DuBois, says Streetcar actor', *The Guardian*, 2 June 2014)

a) To what extent do you agree that Blanche feels 'alien in her surroundings'?

b) What do you think are the advantages and disadvantages of casting a performer with a visible disability in the role of Blanche?

Activity 5

Below is a comparison of the 2002 National Theatre production of the play with the 2014 Young Vic production. After reading it, copy and complete the table.

In the 2002 production, Glenn Close plays an almost comically exaggerated southern belle who enters wearing a large wide-brimmed hat and carries a little white suitcase. Although vulnerable at times, she has an underlying strength. In Scene 10, she fights off Stanley, who is played by the relatively calm, noble Iain Glen. Standing across the room from her, he announces solemnly, 'We've had this date with each other from the beginning!' Close continues to whimper and struggles to get away from him as he approaches and grabs her. In the final scene, she retains some strength, e.g. she makes her final exit through the poker players followed by the Doctor, only taking his arm at the very end. In contrast, in the updated 2014 version, Gillian Anderson's Blanche undergoes a dramatic transition from the witty, stylish woman of the first scene. In Scene 10, she is seen getting into her fancy dress and clumsily smearing her lipstick. The muscular and tattooed Ben Foster plays a particularly brutal Stanley. Blanche falls into a faint in his arms and he then crouches over her, ape-like, throwing her underskirts over her face. In the scene change to Scene 11, Blanche showers and dresses, while the other actors expressionlessly tidy the rooms. Blanche is shattered, her hair is damp, her make-up messy. She teeters on her heels and clings desperately to the Doctor's arm as she leaves.

	2002 Production	2014 Production
Interpretation of Blanche		
Interpretation of Stanley		
Staging of the rape scene		
Staging of the ending		

Writing about performance

Upgrade

When writing about performance, consider how:

- particular casting influences your understanding of a character
- key moments can be interpreted by different designers, actors or directors
- the design of the set can highlight themes and ideas of the play
- radical reinterpretations of the script, e.g. updating the time period or altering the gender of characters, can bring advantages and disadvantages
- performance choices reflect the interests and concerns of the audience.

Academics and critics analyse works of literature from various perspectives. For example, they may study the work seeking to discover attitudes towards gender, politics or language. Awareness of different critical opinions can help you to demonstrate your understanding of different readers' opinions and how a piece of literature is open to interpretation. This chapter covers just a few of the critical stances from which *A Streetcar Named Desire* has been analysed.

Feminist criticism

Influenced by feminism and the impulse to reconsider women's role in society, feminist critics often focus on:

- strong or transgressive female characters
- examples of women's place within the **patriarchy**
- re-examination of assumptions about the roles women play
- examining and challenging the language used to describe femininity and female roles
- comparing the contextual expectation of characters with those of the present day.

A feminist critic may offer an alternative reading of a text in which a female character has been misread, judged or stereotyped, in order to offer a richer or alternative view of that character and the society in which she lives.

Below is an excerpt of an alternative reading of the character of Eunice from a feminist critical perspective, offered by Philip C. Kolin:

> Eunice, I believe, has been stereotyped and thereby marginalized for two reasons: her so-called comic, minor role and her insistent femininity, attributes that **canonical**, patriarchal readings of *Streetcar* have used to dismiss or refute Eunice's importance…I maintain that Eunice's role in Streetcar is neither minor nor predominantly comic; and far from being an accomplice in Stanley's brutal treatment of Blanche, Eunice is a central figure in directing our attention to its horror… Eunice is at the focal point of those issues that are most sacred to Williams: tenderness of heart, solicitude for self and others, and a sense of community.
>
> (Philip C. Kolin, 'Eunice Hubbel and the feminist thematics of *A Streetcar Named Desire*', *Confronting Tennessee Williams's A Streetcar Named Desire: Essays in Critical Pluralism*)

canonical authorized or accepted works; agreed to be important

patriarchy a society which is ruled by men

Activity 1

a) Decide whether or not you agree with Kolin's view of Eunice and supply examples to support your point of view.

b) Read the excerpt below from Felicia Hardison's essay and write your own paragraph arguing for or against the idea that Blanche has an 'emotional dependence' on the patriarchy throughout the play.

This scene [Scene 4] invites feminist criticism: although Blanche regards Stella's husband as a brutal predator, her first impulse is to turn to another man as saviour. There is a subtle irony in her reflexive reversion to the Southern belle's habits of thought – that is, emotional dependence on a patriarchal system of male protection for the helpless female – just moments after she has said, 'I'm going to do something. Get hold of myself and make myself a new life.'

(Felicia Hardison Londre, 'A streetcar running fifty years', *The Cambridge Companion to Tennessee Williams*)

Tips for assessment

You do not have to agree with a critic's point of view, but you must be able to explain why you do or do not accept their interpretation of an idea. It is important to include evidence from the play to support your arguments.

Gender criticism and queer theory

Gender criticism looks beyond feminist concerns to explore constructions of gender and sexuality. It does not focus so much on the idea of patriarchy, with men dominating women, but instead considers how society, through its culture, politics and language, categorizes and prioritizes different individuals and groups. Queer theory developed from the gay liberation movements of the latter half of the 20th century and the term 'queer theory' was introduced in 1990. It seeks to:

- challenge traditional representations of femininity and masculinity
- uncover coded messages about sexuality
- seek out transgressive or anarchic sexual roles
- consider how the sexuality of the writer has influenced the text.

Some critics have explored the possibility that Blanche DuBois is a stand-in for Tennessee Williams himself and his own feelings as a gay man, an outsider and misunderstood by the society of his time. Some directors have taken this idea to its logical conclusion and created productions in which Blanche is played by a man.

The writer below explores how Blanche does not conform to the societal gender norms of the time:

In *A Streetcar Named Desire* (1947), Blanche DuBois can play the prim Southern belle, but her proudest moment is ravishing the soldiers from the nearby base, leaving them spent on the grass where 'later the paddy wagon would gather them up like daisies'. Blanche is a wild card in the seven card stud game that is the sex/gender system.

(John M. Clum, 'The sacrificial stud and the fugitive female in *Suddenly Last Summer*, *Orpheus Descending* and *Sweet Birth of Youth*', *The Cambridge Companion to Tennessee Williams*)

Structuralism

Structuralism is a type of literary criticism that analyses the narrative structure and seeks to uncover patterns. A key concept of structuralism is **binary opposition**, which seeks to identify the **dichotomies** and conflicts between different groups. For example, in *A Streetcar Named Desire*, some binary oppositions include:

- male/female
- working class/landed gentry
- cruelty/kindness
- birth/death
- real/imagined.

The male/female dynamic in the 2002 National Theatre production, with Glenn Close and Iain Glen playing the lead roles

The critic Nancy Tischler writes about these oppositions in Williams's work:

> For Tennessee Williams, the world was the scene of epic battles – between the Flesh and the Spirit, Good and Evil, God and Satan, Gentle Jesus and Terrifying Jehovah.
>
> (Nancy M. Tischler, 'Romantic textures in Williams's plays and short stories', *The Cambridge Companion to Tennessee Williams*)

Activity 2

Use a table like the one below to find examples of binary oppositions in the play (the first few have been suggested for you).

Binary oppositions		Evidence
Wealth	Poverty	
Male	Female	
Birth	Death	

Political or Marxist criticism

Marxist literary criticism takes its inspiration from the writings of socialist philosophers Karl Marx (1818–1883) and Friedrich Engels (1820–1895), and analyses texts by identifying class wars, power struggles and oppression. Marxist critics might consider:

- **capitalism** versus **socialism**
- the role of the **proletariat** and the ruling class
- shifts in power and dominance.

binary opposition concepts or groups of people who can be considered opposites of one another

capitalism a political system which encourages private trade and industry for profit

dichotomies plural of dichotomy; the contrast between starkly different things or opposing forces

proletariat a collective term for working-class people

socialism a political system which promotes state ownership of industry and aims to empower the working class

Below are selected excerpts from a Marxist analysis of *A Streetcar Named Desire* by the critic Robert Bray:

> Viewed in terms of the other characters' actions and motives, then, Blanche may be seen as the ultimate outsider, positioned outside of time, social order, and place. Furthermore, the society that she represents, southern plantation, gives way to the mechanistic grit and grind of the factory, and her psychological death at the play's end must be seen as a victory for the oppressors and the new order that they represent. In this play, at least, the proletariat becomes the ruling class.
>
> Stanley's rudimentary understanding of politics suggests his belief in the quasisocialist system that Long was advocating, with the closest thing the South has ever had to a viable national socialist candidate. Stanley's disgust over Blanche's aristocratic pretensions, his reference to her as 'Her Majesty' and 'visiting Royalty' thus uphold his veneration of Long's populist ideals and phraseology.
>
> The image of the proletarian Stanley pulling Stella 'down off them columns' signifies his furious contempt for that very powerful symbol of landed aristocracy, the Greek revival columns.
>
> (Robert Bray, 'A Streetcar Named Desire – the political and historical subtext', *Confronting Tennessee Williams's A Streetcar Named Desire: Essays in Critical Pluralism*)

Activity 3

Looking particularly at Scene 2, complete the spider diagram below with details from the play which focus on the areas of interest to a Marxist critic.

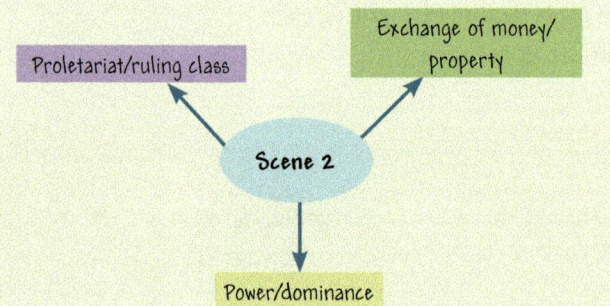

Reader response criticism

Reader response criticism highlights the interaction between a reader and a text. It highlights the creative input of the reader/audience in the creation of a work of art. These critics look for:

- active responses from audiences/readers
- occasions when different audiences/readers may respond differently to a text
- fluctuations in the audience's/reader's response, such as shifting sympathy
- the actual experience of the reader/audience when reading/seeing the text.

The critic June Schlueter offers an example of Reader Response criticism when she considers how the reader of *A Streetcar Named Desire* must choose between the 'competing narratives' of Blanche and Stanley. Readers might also re-evaluate what they previously thought of the characters after their climactic confrontation in Scene 10. Schlueter analyses how in the early scenes Blanche is attempting to create an admirable past for herself while Stanley aims to 'deconstruct' her past. His actions in Scene 10 are the ultimate imposition of his reading of her character and rewriting of her narrative.

Activity 4

Consider your own reaction as a reader of *A Streetcar Named Desire* and try to analyse your own response by answering the following questions.

a) Did your sympathy for the characters shift as you read the play?

b) When you first read the text, were you making certain predictions which did or did not come true?

c) How did you resolve the contradictions within the characters, e.g Blanche's apparent primness and promiscuity?

d) Did you respond differently to the text when you saw it in performance (on stage or on film) rather than reading it?

e) After Scene 10, did you view the characters of Stanley, Blanche and Stella differently?

f) Did you feel that as a 21st-century reader, your response to the text was different from that of an audience in 1947?

Psychological literary criticism

Some critics have been influenced by the psychoanalytical writings of Sigmund Freud (1856–1939) and more recent psychological theories. They seek to use the language and concepts of analysis in literary criticism. Some areas of interest include:

- how the biography of the author might influence the text
- analysis of symbols and what they say about the characters' psychological state
- family dynamics
- hidden or subconscious meanings
- the behaviour of characters that can be explained by psychological concepts such as obsession, neurosis, narcissism and repression.

Activity 5

Read this student's attempt at offering a psychological reading of Blanche and then add at least three sentences to complete it, providing evidence from the play.

> Blanche is a complex character who is fighting her inner demons. She has a strong sexual drive as demonstrated by her behaviour towards the soldiers in Laurel, her young student and the young newspaper collector. Yet she also realizes the importance of repressing her desires, apparently separating her sexual needs with her desire for safety which she views as achievable only in marriage. Additionally, her traumatic experiences caused by the death of her husband and the nursing of her dying family have left her psychologically damaged, causing her to self-medicate with alcohol. In modern analysis she might be diagnosed as suffering from **post-traumatic stress disorder**.

post-traumatic stress disorder (PTSD) a condition in which someone who has experienced a violent, shocking or frightening event relives the experience through flashbacks or nightmares, and experiences other symptoms such as feelings of guilt and isolation

Writing about critical views

To improve your writing about different critical responses to the text, try the following:

- Don't just quote a critic but have the confidence to extend their ideas or disagree with them.

- Read critical opinions which are contradictory, weigh them up and decide which you most agree with and why.

- Choose a scene and analyse it yourself from different critical perspectives.

- Consider what we know about the characters' families, and how that understanding could enrich a psychological reading of the text.

- Reflect on what we know about the characters' attitudes towards money and how that could influence a Marxist reading of the text.

- If you are quoting a critic, make sure you acknowledge them.

- Don't take credit for ideas that aren't yours, but do build on and interact with other writers' ideas.

- Remember you do not have to agree entirely with a critic. It is important that you understand different viewpoints but develop your own ideas.

Exam skills

A key to exam success is practice. Take advantage of any opportunities to study past papers and undertake timed writing. Many students find the demands of writing under tight time constraints challenging, but this gets easier with training.

Understanding the question

It is important that you carefully read the question and underline key words and phrases to make sure that you steer your response in the correct direction. Some questions may be extract-based, directing you to respond to a particular section of the text, while others will be focused on character, theme, genre or context. No matter what the question, you will need to demonstrate that you can write about language, structure and form.

Character-based question

'The <u>relationship</u> between <u>Stanley</u> and <u>Stella</u> is an example of the <u>attraction of opposites</u>.' <u>To what extent</u> do you agree with this statement?

The focus of this question is the relationship between Stanley and Stella. This gives you the opportunity to write about their different backgrounds and attitudes, but also what binds them together. Remember that 'to what extent' means that you do not have to totally agree or disagree with the original statement – you are weighing up the evidence and coming to a conclusion.

Theme-based question

'<u>Light</u> serves many functions in the play.' Choose <u>several key moments</u> when the <u>symbolic use of light</u> illuminates a <u>particular theme</u> and analyse its <u>importance</u>.

This question requires an understanding of a number of things: symbolism, themes and plot. Key moments you could analyse include: Scene 3 when Mitch helps Blanche with the paper lantern; the candlelight in Scene 6; Scene 9 when Mitch shines the light in Blanche's face; and Scene 11 when Stanley presents the broken lantern to Blanche.

Context-based question

> 'A *Streetcar Named Desire* could only have been written in the <u>1940s</u>.'
> Analyse the play with reference to how it portrays the <u>interests</u> and
> <u>concerns of the time</u>.

You must select specific aspects of the play's 1940s context to analyse. Some fruitful lines of inquiry might include post-Second World War, new social order, the dying South or gender roles. However, you must make sure your analysis includes a literary analysis of key moments, such as Stanley's Huey Long speech or the moment he hits Stella.

Genre-based question

> 'How does Williams's use of <u>comedy</u> help to convey the <u>characters</u> and
> their <u>feelings</u> and <u>attitudes</u> in the play?'

You should identify the purpose of comedy in the play and what it reveals about the characters of Blanche and Stanley. You could explore moments when the characters create comic effects both intentionally and unintentionally. This question offers the opportunity to discuss irony and genre.

Extract-based question

> Looking closely at <u>Scene 3</u>, starting with 'Blanche: Hello! The Little
> Boys' Room…' to the end of the scene, analyse the importance of the
> character of <u>Mitch</u>, including his use of <u>language</u> and his <u>relationships</u>
> with the other characters.

Mitch's language contrasts with Blanche's more sophisticated and literary style, revealing his simple, sensitive nature, through his relationship with the dead girl and his ill mother. He can also be examined in relation to the other poker players, who tease him, and Blanche, who immediately considers him a possible suitor.

Planning your answer

Given time constraints, it is tempting just to launch into writing your answer without making a plan. However, a common feature of successful answers is evidence of planning. Plans help you to organize your ideas and make sure that you don't leave out important points. There is not one 'right' way of making a plan, but some techniques include bullet point lists, spider diagrams and paragraph plans. Below is a sample question with three different plans for a response.

> 'The past poisons the present.' To what extent do you agree with this statement in relation to the play *A Streetcar Named Desire*?

Bullet point list

Past

- Belle Reve
- Allan Grey
- Thrown out of Laurel
- Genre: tragedy – haunted by the past
- Quotations: 'Yes, it was – a pretty long time ago' (Scene 7)
- 'There are thousands of papers, stretching back over hundreds of years, affecting Belle Reve as, piece by piece, our improvident grandfathers and father and uncles and brothers exchanged the land for their epic fornications' (Scene 2)

Present

- New Orleans
- Stanley
- Context: post-Second World War, immigrants versus landed gentry
- Quotations: 'I pulled you down off them columns and how you loved it, having them coloured lights going!' (Scene 8)

Conclusion

- Blanche destroyed by her inability to deal with the past

Spider diagram

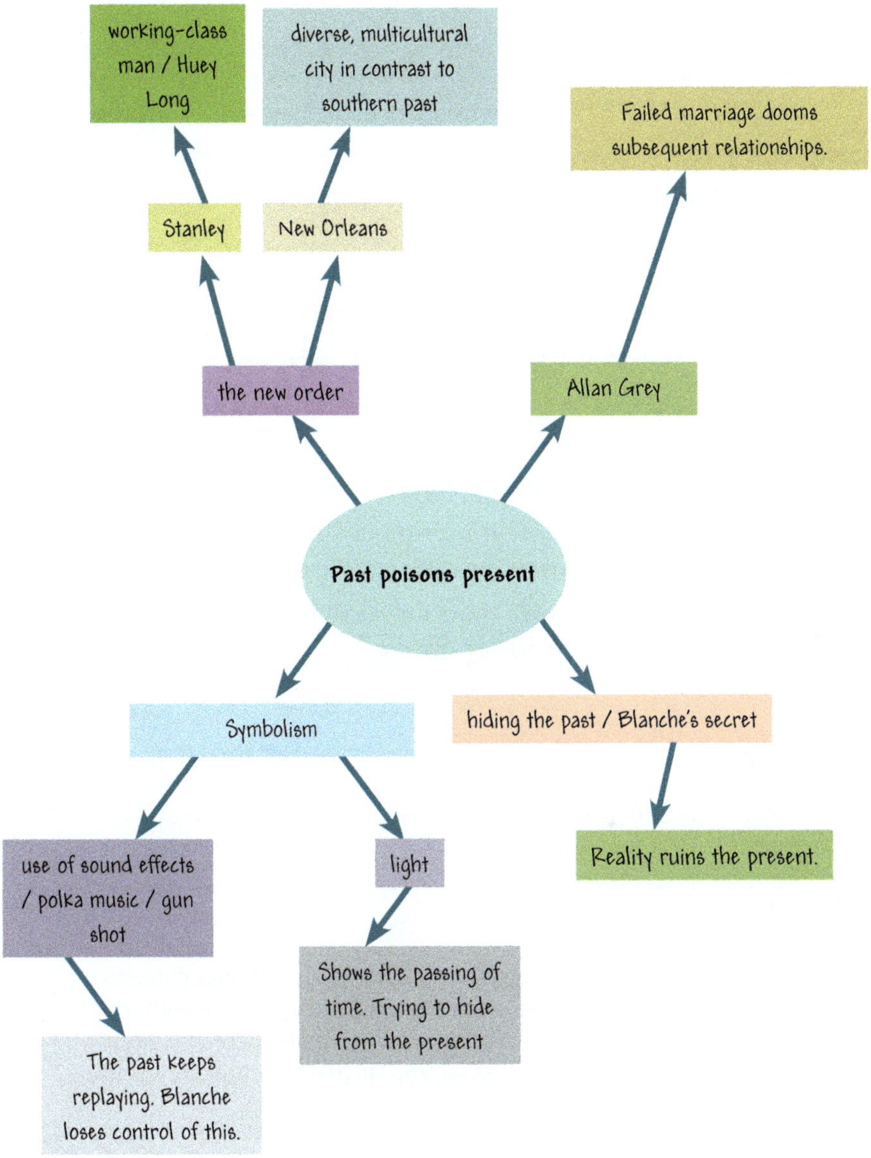

working-class man / Huey Long

diverse, multicultural city in contrast to southern past

Failed marriage dooms subsequent relationships.

Stanley

New Orleans

the new order

Allan Grey

Past poisons present

Symbolism

hiding the past / Blanche's secret

use of sound effects / polka music / gun shot

light

Reality ruins the present.

The past keeps replaying. Blanche loses control of this.

Shows the passing of time. Trying to hide from the present

Activity 1

Using the spider diagram above, add specific quotations to support key points.

Tips for assessment

When using lists or diagrams as a planning method, consider numbering your ideas so that you work through them in an effective order. Put a tick next to a point as you make it, so you avoid making it twice or leaving it out altogether.

Paragraph plan

Introduction Blanche arrives carrying the baggage of her past: husband's suicide; loss of Belle Reve and job; past indiscretions. She is seeking a new future, but clings to the past.

Paragraph 1 Belle Reve: context, southern land owning versus new urban reality.

Paragraph 2 Marriage: revelation of her sad past marriage brings her hope of a new present happiness with Mitch. (Scene 6)

Paragraph 3 Secrets: revelation of her past destroys her relationship with Mitch. (Scene 9)

Paragraph 4 Inability to separate past from present: mental instability. Use of expressionist stage techniques to convey her fragile grasp. 'spectral admirers' in Scene 10.

Conclusion Blanche's tragic downfall. Shame and humiliation. (Scene 11) The cruelty of the present destroying a fragile person like Blanche.

Activity 2

Experiment with these different methods of planning by creating three different styles of plan for the following question:

'Stella is torn between her husband and sister, but eventually chooses her own survival above all else.' To what extent do you agree with this statement? Write about the character of Stella, remembering to include observations about the context, as well as language, form and structure.

Tips for assessment

Although it is important to make a plan, remember it should be done quickly. It should be written in note form, not full paragraphs.

Writing your answer

Structuring your response

Although there are no set rules about how to structure your essay, some students find it helpful to think of their response using a template like this:

Introduction: Opening argument

Paragraph 1: at least three points with supporting examples and analysis

Paragraph 2: at least three points with supporting examples and analysis

Paragraph 3: at least three points with supporting examples and analysis

Conclusion: bring points together and arrive at a final conclusion.

When practising your answers, guidance like this can be helpful as it reminds you to support your ideas with evidence and analysis, but it can be restricting. For example, you may wish to write more than five paragraphs or you may have a wide-ranging series of points you wish to make, so don't feel bound by this. However, using a template for revision and planning practice can increase your confidence in your ability to structure a response quickly.

Tips for assessment

Use some of the wording of the question in your first paragraph and subsequent paragraphs as this will help to keep you on topic and reassure the examiner that you have understood the focus of the question.

Prioritizing your ideas

A common error in essay writing is to give all points equal weight, which lessens the sense of a well-shaped, thoughtful argument. In order to avoid this try to use **discourse markers** to guide the reader through your response. Examples include the following words and phrases:

- **To introduce order:** first; in the beginning; next; subsequently; finally.
- **To prioritize or emphasize:** most importantly; significantly; notably; especially.
- **To suggest comparisons or contrasts:** alternatively; on the other hand; in contrast; similarly; in the same way; equally.

discourse marker 'signpost' words or phrases which help to direct the reader to the order, importance or relationship of ideas being presented

Activity 3

Write a paragraph contrasting your first impressions of the characters of Blanche and Stanley, using at least three discourse markers to clarify your ideas.

Developing an academic writing style

Below is an example of a student's writing which demonstrates some difficulties in assuming an academic register:

When I first read the play I really didn't like Blanche and was surprised to learn that she was going to be the main character in the play. She seemed snobby and isn't nice at all to Eunice, who is only trying to help her. I was interested when she began talking about the streetcars because I'd never heard of streetcars with those names, so I assumed that Williams was putting some serious symbolism into the play. He probably wanted us to be intrigued by what wasn't really a very interesting beginning to the play. I could tell that Blanche was supposed to be an outsider because she was dressed differently from everyone else, all in white.

Activity 4

Read an examiner's comments on this piece of writing below and then rewrite the paragraph with the improvements suggested.

Examiner's comments

- Too great a use of 'I'. A response should not just rely on personal opinions and first impressions.

- Write about the characters as constructions of the playwright, not as real people.

- Vocabulary is too informal, e.g. 'snobby,' or too simple, e.g. 'nice.'

- Does attempt some literary terminology, e.g. 'symbolism', but doesn't really analyse this beyond suggesting that we might be 'intrigued'.

- Identifies an important idea that Blanche is an outsider, but could develop this further.

- All ideas are given equal weight; there is no ordering or prioritizing.

Using quotations

Key to your success is your ability to select and analyse quotations from the play in order to support your argument. Ideally, your examples should be brief and embedded in a grammatically correct way into your writing. For example:

> Eunice may be depicted as a comic character, constantly arguing and making up with the wandering Steve. Despite her apparent kindness to Stella, Stella jokingly refers to her in Scene 3 as 'that one upstairs' and laughs. The phrase 'that one' removes the friendly neighbourliness assumed by Eunice's actions in Scene 1 and pits Blanche and Stella against what they perceive as a different class of woman. Eunice continues to be a source of humour in Scene 5 when, after a noisy fight with Steve ('a clatter of aluminium striking a wall is heard'), she goes to the bar rather than the police. She is depicted as a character who has few boundaries and lives her life very publicly.

Activity 5

The student below wants to analyse Mitch's role, but has struggled with embedding short quotations. Read the response and then rewrite it so that the quotations are shorter, presented more correctly and clearly analysed.

> In Scene 9, the audience sees a different side to Mitch. For example, he suddenly wants to see Blanche in the light. He says, 'I've asked you to go out with me sometimes on Sundays but you always make an excuse. You never want to go out till after six and then it's always some place that's not lighted much.' This shows that he has begun to figure out that Blanche has been hiding something from him. He says, 'Oh, I knew you weren't sixteen any more. But I was a fool enough to believe you was straight.' (Scene 9) This shows how shocked he was by Stanley's revelation.

Tips for assessment

Remember that not all your quotations in an answer have to be long. A quotation can occasionally be as short as a single word. An analysis of a well-chosen word is worth more than longer, unanalysed quotations.

Citing critics and other readers' opinions

You may wish to refer to the opinions of others in your essay. It is important that you make it clear when words are not your own. For example, you might write:

> As the writer Robert Bray stated, the play's ending must be 'seen as a victory for the oppressors and the new order that they represent'. However, in my opinion, many audiences may see this as an uneasy victory.

If you do not have a critic that you specifically want to quote or cite, you can instead evaluate a general critical position or adopt a critical stance yourself. For example:

> Stella can hardly been seen as a **feminist icon** with her readiness to side with her husband against her sister and her meek acceptance of the roles of wife and mother. However, feminist critics might note little acts of rebellion from Stella: her criticism of the poker game; her enjoyment of going out; her guilt at Blanche's exit. It may be that in this male-dominated society, she is simply a realist.

> **feminist icon** someone who is a positive role model for women, e.g. by a show of strength, intelligence or independence beyond what is expected in her society

Activity 6

a) Memorize a few key quotations from reviews of the play and academic articles.

b) Choose a question and write a paragraph, adopting a critical stance using the quotations you have memorized.

Sample questions

Opposite are examples of the style of questions that you might be asked in the exam with some of the typical wording. Notice that one type of question is to make a statement and then ask if you agree with it. Remember that in those instances you do not need to agree whole-heartedly with the statement, but you should find and analyse evidence which either supports or disagrees with it. Other questions might direct you to a particular scene or excerpt or focus on a theme or character. In all instances, you will be required to write in a fluent, knowledgeable way about the play and show that you can analyse the relevant sections of the play using correct literary terminology.

1 'Despite the emphasis on Blanche's dilemma, Mitch is the true victim of the play.' How far do you agree with this statement?

2 Starting your discussion with a detailed analysis of the end of Scene 4, examine the view that *A Streetcar Named Desire* is a play about the war between social classes.

3 '*A Streetcar Named Desire* is a play influenced more by death than desire.' In the light of this comment, analyse the presentation of death and desire in the play. Remember to include contextual elements in your answer.

4 Examine the role of Eunice in the play and how Williams uses her character to reveal the play's themes and concerns.

5 How does Williams use symbolism to expose the character of Blanche?

6 Referring closely to Scene 6, how does Williams expose the concerns and prejudices of the time? In your answer, you must also consider the language, form and structure of the play.

Activity 7

Use the sample questions above to practise your planning and writing skills.

Tips for assessment

Use the following checklist to evaluate and improve your work:

- Have you made clear from your first paragraph that you are answering the question?
- Have you used some of the wording of the question in your answer?
- Have you used quotations to support your ideas?
- Have you used clear linking phrases and discourse markers?
- Have you considered how the play's context could influence your understanding of it?
- Have you used correct terminology, such as: protagonist, tragedy, dialogue, stage directions, symbolism, characterization?
- Have you considered other interpretations or opinions?
- Have you made a number of different points, rather than repeating the same ones?
- Have you checked that your spelling, grammar and punctuation are correct?

Sample answers

Sample answer 1

> 'All the female characters in the play are ultimately shown by Williams to be victims of a male-dominated society.' To what extent do you agree with this statement?

Williams was highly aware of the fragility of women's roles in 1940s society. Two influences on his writing of 'A Streetcar Named Desire' were his mother, a frustrated southern belle, who keenly felt the financial hardships to which her family was sometimes exposed and his sister Rose, who suffered from mental illness for much of her life. The women in his life experienced a lack of opportunity to express themselves in a creative, useful way and instead resorted to fantasies, failed aspirations and, in the case of Rose, insanity. Similarly, in 'A Streetcar Named Desire' the limited range of opportunities clearly has an effect on the lives of Stella, Eunice and, most significantly, Blanche, and all could be considered victims of a male-dominated society, which values physical strength and the ability to earn money in pursuit of the American Dream.

Relevant contextual information.

Uses some of the wording from the question to avoid straying off topic.

After the Second World War, the expectation was that women would provide a welcoming home for the returning soldiers. Stella, having escaped from the restrictions of the decaying Belle Reve, meets Stanley, who has served in the armed forces. His uniform blurs his status, though she insists to Blanche that she was not 'blinded by all the brass'. Nevertheless, she admits that she had to 'adjust' herself, with apparently all accommodations being made on her side, rather than Stanley's. Stanley's domination is clear when he quotes Huey Long, declaring 'Every Man is a King!' It is significant that it is the status of men that this declaration reinforces, with the assumption that it is Stella's role to cook, serve and clean, while Stanley handles all the money. Stanley's physical dominance over Stella is reinforced when he hits her in Scene 3, lifts her off her feet at the end of Scene 3 and, metaphorically, when he declares that he 'pulled' her 'down off them columns'. The 'columns' symbolize Belle Reve, Stella's ancestral home and the act of pulling her down is full of violence and excitement. She has surrendered not only physically to him, but also by abandoning her upbringing and past.

An abrupt start. Could use a better link to the previous paragraph.

Uses appropriate quotation with some analysis.

A number of points made concisely with clear evidence from text.

Useful analysis of text, which connects well to question.

On the other hand, Eunice seems to be a more equal match for Steve, who may try to dominate her but is also at the receiving end of Eunice's sharp tongue and strong arm. However, her life too is limited. She is seen on the street around the apartment and can console herself at the local bar, but she lacks the freedom of Steve, who she accuses of chasing a blonde round the balcony. Steve has his bowling nights, his blonde, his poker nights and his job, while Eunice expends her energy gossiping and performing household tasks. The critic Philip C. Kolin views Eunice with particular sympathy, highlighting her 'tenderness of heart' and 'sense of community'. It is as if she is the choral figure who directs the audience's attention to the tragedy which befalls Blanche and she is also the pragmatic friend who reassures Stella that she has made the only possible choice. It may be that the audience is wrong to consider her comic, but should admire her insistence that 'Life has got to go on'. This realistic line gives her a certain dignity in contrast to the comic angry wife of the earlier scenes, showing her unwillingness to be totally dominated or defeated by a patriarchal society.

Shows confidence to quote a critic and then extend those ideas.

It is Blanche who most clearly fights against the expectations of a woman in the 1940s, though she is also probably the least suited for such a battle. Her first marriage could be seen as a rejection of a marriage dominated by a man. In the coded language of the 1940s, in Scene 6, she speaks of being married, not to a man but 'a boy, just a boy'. Instead of dominating her, he came to her for help. Williams uses the metaphor, 'He was in the quicksands and clutching at me', which suggests not only his lack of dominance, but also his desperation. It could be argued that they were both victims of the rigid gender expectations of the time. The 'disgust' that Blanche felt for him was shared by that of society at large and her expression of it confirmed his agony, leading to his suicide.

Suggestion of applying theoretical analysis, but could be extended.

Another scene which challenges typical gender roles is Scene 5, in which Blanche assumes the role of sexual predator towards the Young Man. However, Blanche performs more to expectations in Scene 6 when she flirts with Mitch, while denying him sexual satisfaction, which can only be won by a commitment to marriage. Having lost her job and her family's inheritance, she has turned to the only possibility of salvation – marriage.

Although the women in the play have lives which an audience might now find constricted and demeaning, it would be simplistic to say that it was only women who suffered under these rigid rules. Mitch suffers as an unmarried man looking after his ill mother and Allan Grey suffered by having to keep his sexuality a secret. Williams seems to be speaking up for all who are unconventional or outcasts, and therefore unable to survive in a cruel world which rewards only the fittest.

Although some points, including those in the final two paragraphs, could use more development and appropriate quotations from the play, there is much evidence of understanding and analysis, including use of literary terminology like 'metaphor' and the ability to quote a critic. A little more emphasis on language and stagecraft would improve this further, but overall a commendable response.

Sample answer 2

> 'In Stanley, Williams created a new sort of hero for a new society.'
> Discuss this statement, remembering to include any relevant contextual
> information.

In the film of the play, Marlon Brando introduced a new sort of hero to cinema audiences. He was dressed casually and his mumbling, off-hand style contrasted to the more prim, precise performance by Vivien Leigh as Blanche. Stanley continues to be a character who fascinates actors and audiences. He is a working-class man who dominates the stage with his physicality, humour and determination. In some productions he actually overwhelms what Williams's stated intentions were, causing audiences to sympathize more with him than with the supposed protagonist of the play, Blanche.

Not clear from this opening that the question is going to be answered.

Although true, this paragraph does not suggest the argument of the response.

An actor playing Stanley needs to understand the positive aspects of his character. He comes from immigrant stock but is proudly 'one hundred per cent American'. He served in the army as a 'Master Sergeant in the Engineers' Corps' and must have done well as he was decorated. He holds down a job and Stella believes that he will do well because he has 'drive'. He loves Stella and is excited about the birth of their child. To see the play from his point of view, it is unreasonable to expect to put up his alcoholic sister-in-law for an unlimited amount of time in such a tiny apartment. He could also be uneasy with Blanche's flirtatious ways, such as spraying him with perfume or asking him to do up her buttons. So it is fair to say, that an audience could look at him as the hero of the play, who is just doing what he needs to in order to protect his family and lifestyle.

Shows some understanding, but doesn't write about the characters as constructions. Needs to consider literary techniques.

An important scene for understanding Stanley is Scene 2, when he discovers that Belle Reve has been 'lost'. In this scene, Stanley can be seen standing up for his rights as a husband. It is not unreasonable that he wants more explanation than just Blanche's words. Even Blanche seems to acknowledge that he has a point when she says, 'But maybe he's what we need to mix with our blood now that we've lost Belle Reve and have to go on without Belle Reve to protect us.' Blanche's expectation is that a masculine figure like Stanley is needed to 'protect' them now that their wealth won't.

An appropriate quotation, but needs analysis to connect to the question.

It might have been better to have started with a version of this paragraph as it suggests some key ideas about the play.

A big point of conflict in the play is the difference between Blanche and Stanley. Blanche represents the 'old order', the South, the gentry, literature and etiquette. Stanley represents the 'new order' with the 'drive' to succeed, the working-class energy and the emphasis on surviving in a tough world. He isn't educated like Blanche, but he is more cunning and knows how to get his way. Williams shows this by having Stanley misunderstand things like what a 'rhinestone' is and by his use of unconventional sociolect when he speaks.

At the end of the play, it is Stanley who is clearly the victor. He has not only won by getting rid of Blanche, but he is, in contrast to Scene 3, suddenly winning at poker. He declares that 'Luck is believing that you're lucky' and that could be his motto. His self-belief is what carries him through the play. He is convinced that he will win Stella and win in life.

This is too informal. A more academic approach throughout would help this answer improve its focus and analysis.

So yes, I would agree that Tennessee Williams has created a new hero, who, although not always sympathetic, is the sort of character who can survive and succeed in the tough urban American society. It isn't a time to be polite or intellectual, but instead it is a time for tough-mindedness and determination, even if it means the destruction of the old order as represented by Blanche. In the end, Stella must choose between Stanley and Blanche, and, although she feels guilty, the final stage directions show who she has chosen – Stanley.

This response would have been greatly improved by a clear plan and closer focus on the question. From the first paragraph, there is a sense of wandering from the actual question and this continues throughout much of the essay. Although it is fine to reference the film, remember you must analyse the play and offer insight into its use of language.

Sample answer 3

'Williams was speaking on behalf of anyone who was an outsider.'
Explore this statement in relation to the play *A Streetcar Named Desire*.

Tennessee Williams was known for passionately siding with the lonely and unconventional. Through his own personal experiences, as a gay man in the 1940s, he knew what it felt like to fall outside typical societal expectations. Throughout 'A Streetcar Named Desire' he gives voice to those who do not conform and reveals the price they pay for being outsiders. In addition to Blanche, the play's tragic protagonist, the off-stage character of Allan Grey is also an outsider, as is, to a lesser extent, Mitch.

Relevant, accurate context introduced and linked to question.

A concise introduction, suggesting the nature of the argument.

Blanche is portrayed as an outsider, 'incongruous' in New Orleans, from the first scene of the play. Through his stage directions, Williams establishes the vivid, multicultural New Orleans setting, which contrasts with the delicate, moth-like Blanche, who arrives dressed entirely in white 'as if she were arriving at a summer tea'. A sense of the New Orleans community is established through the joking and gossip of Eunice and the Negro Woman, and Stanley's crude throwing of the meat to a laughing Stella. Against this backdrop, Blanche seems too fragile to survive. Williams uses adjectives like 'delicate' and 'uncertain' to emphasize her vulnerability. She has entered a world of which the rules seem to evade her and she ends up sneaking alcohol, another guilty secret, which contributes to her outsider status, in order to calm her nerves.

Effective analysis of stage directions with well-chosen quotations.

Her outsider role is further confirmed by her uncomfortable relationship with Stanley. She is the unwelcome third member of the household, which had previously been run entirely according to Stanley's needs. Williams highlights the enforced intimacy of the flat by having only thin curtains separating the rooms and making clear that the sounds from the bathroom, such as Blanche's singing, are clearly audible in the other rooms. There is no place for Blanche to hide. By Scene 2, it is evident that Stanley is losing patience with Blanche, accusing her of squandering Belle Reve. However, the turning point in their relationship is at the end of Scene 4 when he overhears her criticisms of him. Blanche attempts to convince Stella of the finer things: 'Such things as art – as poetry and music' in contrast to the brute strength exhibited by Stanley, whom she suggests is 'ape-like'. The binary oppositions are established: Blanche versus Stanley; art versus strength; imagination versus reality.

Demonstrates understanding of structure, including turning point.

Suggests structuralist approach by noting binary oppositions.

In some productions of the play, Blanche's outsider status is sometimes emphasized by casting choices. In a 2014 production, a disabled actress played the role, which was said to emphasize the idea of Blanche being 'alien', while another production played with the outsider status by having a 'drag artist' play Blanche. However, even when traditionally cast, Blanche's difference is conveyed by Williams's heightened dialogue, Blanche's sense of performance and the expressionistic stage directions depicting all the memories that haunt her.

Considers form and style by referring to expressionistic stage directions, though this could be demonstrated rather than simply stated.

However, Blanche is not the only outsider in the play. Her husband Allan Grey was unable to conform to the expectations of 1940s men. He is described by Stella as 'a boy who wrote poetry' (interestingly both Stella and Blanche refer to him as a 'boy' rather than as a man) who was discovered to be a 'degenerate'. With Blanche unable to save him and then denouncing him, he commits suicide, which becomes the defining moment of Blanche's life. In the 1940s, when there were many restrictions on homosexuals, Williams's treatment of Allan Grey's story, even though it occurs before the play began, was considered groundbreaking, an early breakthrough in telling stories which are frequently repressed.

Relevant contextual and theoretical approach.

Mitch too could be considered an outsider, a single man amongst married couples, who significantly works in the 'spare parts' department. His only known previous relationship was with a dying girl. She too could be conferred outsider status, as Mitch refers to her as 'a very strange girl, very sweet – very!' Like Blanche and Allan Grey, she seems to have enjoyed an interest in literature, as she has two lines from a poem inscribed on a cigarette case for Mitch, which seems to be one of his proudest possessions. When Mitch proposes to Blanche – 'You need somebody. And I need somebody, too.' – he is acknowledging their mutual loneliness and neediness as much as any passion.

Last paragraph could be further developed.

While watching the play, the audience's sympathy might well fluctuate as Blanche, the outsider, is not always a likable character. She is untruthful, pretentious and self-centred, but by the final scene, there is a nobility to her suffering. She is not strong, the stage directions indicating that her actions are performed 'weakly, hesitantly', but she still has her dreams, as depicted in her speech about dying at sea, and her trusting nature as she clings to the Doctor, depending on his 'kindness'. However, the final image of the play is of Blanche, being removed to the asylum, the ultimate destination for ultimate outsiders, while the Kowalski household carries on.

A number of points concisely made show a confident understanding of the play, its themes and context, as well as possible interpretations. At times the writing could be a little more sophisticated, with more analysis of language, but overall a persuasive and confident piece.

Sample answer 4

> Discuss the significance of 'The Poker Night' in relation to the play as a whole.

'The Poker Night' is the name given to the play's important third scene and was also, for a brief period, the working title of the whole play, so obviously was considered significant by Tennessee Williams. Scene 3 is a rich scene, which highlights many of the play's key themes: masculinity versus femininity; love and marriage; and violence. The events of the scene are important in the development of the audience's understanding of the relationships of Stanley and Stella, and the introduction of Mitch to Blanche. At the play's tragic ending, the poker players reappear, emphasizing their role in the play's action.

A straightforward, efficient opening, although it could have a greater sense of argument.

Williams's stage directions highlight the unique atmosphere of this scene. His use of colours: 'solid blues, a purple, a red-and-white check', contrast with the white worn by Blanche in the first scene and also recall Blanche's reference to her alleged preference for 'strong, bold colours, primary colours' in the previous scene with Stanley. Williams's use of colour-coding throughout the play hints at the moods and personalities of the characters. The primary colours in this scene emphasize the masculinity of the poker players, who are described as being 'at the peak of their physical manhood'. The men have transformed the apartment, which was previously presented as a modest home, into a highly masculine, competitive space. The use of props reinforces this – whisky bottles, watermelon rinds, poker chips and cards.

Some close reading of the use of colours.

The poker game itself has a number of connotations. In Scene 2, Stanley refers to a woman needing to 'Lay … her cards on the table', as indicating his reluctance for subterfuge or evasion. The characters in this scene refer to cards being 'wild', which has implications of being the odd one out or not conforming to the normal rules. The outsider characters in the play, such as Blanche, could be considered 'wild cards'. Moreover, the word 'stud' is undeniably masculine, as befitting the players of the game. Highlighting the themes of masculinity and social class, the men are also playing for money and none of them are in a position to take a loss of money without also losing face.

Makes a number of valid points, but needs more development and shaping.

When Blanche and Stella enter this scene, a conflict between the women and men is introduced. The women are not welcomed into the flat. Instead, Stanley announces that he won't stand up 'so don't be worried',

An opportunity missed here to introduce a theoretical response, such as feminist interpretation.

refuses Blanche's request to 'kibitz' (or look on) and suggests the women go upstairs to Eunice. A dividing line is established by the drawing of the curtains. On one side, the women undertake 'feminine' activities, such as listening to the radio, changing clothes and gossiping, while the men continue their competitive and money-oriented game.

Demonstrates an understanding of the play's structure.

One of the significant actions of the play is Mitch crossing from the masculine side of the flat to the feminine side. Within the poker players, Stanley is the dominant male, while the unmarried Mitch is the 'spare part' who is teased by the others for his concern for his ill mother. The dialogue between Mitch and Blanche, in the highly unromantic location outside the bathroom door, begins the trajectory of their relationship, which peaks in Scene 6 and is destroyed by Scene 9. In this scene, we see a more charming side to Blanche as she draws out information about Mitch's attachment to the now dead girl and she speaks one of her most touching lines: 'The little there is belongs to people who have experienced some sorrow.' It is this idea of shared sorrow which brings them together in Scene 6.

Uses some appropriate literary terminology and connects to the rest of the play.

The climax of the scene occurs when Stanley attacks Stella, which also foreshadows his violence in Scene 10 towards Blanche. However, violence is only one side of Stanley and Stella's relationship. Stella's passionate willingness to forgive Stanley – 'Her eyes go blind with tenderness as she catches his head and raises him level with her' – demonstrates the other. Blanche's subsequent reaction to Stanley's violence and her determination that Stella should try to escape from him sows the seed of the essential conflict between them.

Lapses slightly into retelling the scene, but does select some quotations.

In the final scene of the play, the poker players return, but Stanley, who had been losing at cards in Scene 3, which undoubtedly contributed to his bad mood, is now depicted as being triumphant. His happiness is caused not only by the change in his 'luck' but also by his knowledge that he will soon be rid of his sister-in-law. The presence of the poker players in this scene, which is remarked on by Eunice who calls them 'pigs', emphasizes the callousness of the world and its insensitivity to a fragile creature like Blanche. The female characters have to pass awkwardly through their card game while readying Blanche for the asylum. The final words of the play, 'This game is seven-card stud', demonstrate that Stanley has won this particular game.

This is a good first effort at this question and covers many relevant points. To improve this response, there needs to be a greater analysis of the language of the play, its context and, possibly, use of a critical perspective to underpin points about masculinity.

Glossary

abstract expressionism a post-Second World War art movement based on non-representational, apparently spontaneous work

allusion a figure of speech which references the Bible, a myth or work of literature to comment upon something else

American Dream the idea that every American, whatever his or her background, can achieve prosperity and success through hard work

anomalies unusual or odd cases

antagonist a character who opposes the protagonist

anti-climactic a descent or retreat from the intensity of the climax

antithesis entirely opposite to something or someone

bequeathed left in a will or handed down to a successor

binary opposition concepts or groups of people who can be considered opposites of one another

canonical authorized or accepted works; agreed to be important

capitalism a political system which encourages private trade and industry for profit

catalyst something or someone that starts or initiates an action or event

catharsis the purification or cleansing of emotion

climax the most intense moment

clip joint a bar or nightclub which deceptively overcharges for drinks

comedy of manners a play which mocks the social behaviour of a particular group

connotations ideas or feelings associated with something

denouement the final part of a play or film, when the various plot strands are concluded

dialect pronunciations and word choices used by people of a particular geographical region

dichotomies plural of dichotomy; the contrast between starkly different things or opposing forces

diction choice of words

discourse marker 'signpost' words or phrases which help to direct the reader to the order, importance or relationship of ideas being presented

dramatic irony irony used to make the audience aware of something unknown to the characters

epigraph a quotation at the beginning of a literary work which indicates the concerns or themes that will follow

episodic a series of loosely connected episodes or scenes which may depict a period of time

existentialism a philosophy which focuses on the will of the individual and is associated with a sense of alienation or disorientation in an absurd world

expressionism a 20th-century movement which sought to express emotional experiences in a symbolic, distorted, stylized fashion

falling action the section of the plot between the climax and the resolution, which often focuses on the direct consequences of the climax

feminist icon someone who is a positive role model for women, e.g. by a show of strength, intelligence or independence beyond what is expected in her society

figurative language a variety of literary techniques, such as metaphors and similes, which go beyond the literal meaning of words

foreshadowing a literary device in which the author hints at what will happen at a later point

harbinger something or someone who signals or forecasts something

hyperbole exaggeration

imagery the use of visual or other vivid language to convey ideas or emotions

imperialism using force to extend a country's powers and borders

in the round a theatre configuration where the audience is positioned all around the stage, rather than just in front of it

irony words that express the opposite of what is meant; the difference between what may be expected and what actually occurs

metaphor a figure of speech when two things are compared without using the word 'like' or 'as'

metatheatrical drawing attention to the theatricality of a performance, e.g. having a play-within-a play or a character overtly play-acting; drawing attention to the artificiality of a performance

method acting a system of acting that came into prominence in the 1930s in which actors learn to connect emotionally with the characters they are playing in order to produce realistic and original performances

offstage character a character not seen on stage

pathos encouraging feelings of sorrow and pity

patriarchy a society which is ruled by men

personifying giving human attributes to an idea or object

post-traumatic stress disorder (PTSD) a condition in which someone who has experienced a violent, shocking or frightening event relives the experience through flashbacks or nightmares, and experiences other symptoms such as feelings of guilt and isolation

profane irreverent; disrespectful

proletariat a collective term for working-class people

propriety obeying conventional rules of behaviour

protagonist the central character, who must overcome obstacles in an attempt to achieve a goal

realism presenting life or events without artificiality, aiming for truthfulness

register use of language which changes in formality depending on the situation

ribald crude humour, usually involving jokes about sex

scrims gauze screens which can be opaque or transparent depending on how they are lit

sociolect pronunciations and word choices used by people of a particular social class

socialism a political system which promotes state ownership of industry and aims to empower the working class

southern gothic a genre of fiction set in a decayed, damaged South of the United States. The novels often focus on the grotesque, bizarre or macabre

stage directions written instructions conveying the appearance and actions of the play

subsuming including or absorbing

sub-text an underlying or unspoken meaning

symbolism representing something with something else, such as a cross to represent Christianity or chains to represent enslavement

themes key ideas or recurring subjects which appear in a work of literature

tragic flaw a defect or failing in the tragic protagonist that brings around his or her downfall

tragi-comedy a genre which includes aspects of both comedy and tragedy

transgressive breaking boundaries, rules, social orders or moral codes

OXFORD
UNIVERSITY PRESS

Great Clarendon Street, Oxford, OX2 6DP, United Kingdom

Oxford University Press is a department of the University of Oxford. It furthers the University's objective of excellence in research, scholarship, and education by publishing worldwide. Oxford is a registered trade mark of Oxford University Press in the UK and in certain other countries

British Library Cataloguing in Publication Data

Data available

ISBN 978-019-839900-1

Kindle edition ISBN 978-019-839901-8

10   9

Printed in Great Britain by CPI Group (UK) Ltd., Croydon CR0 4YY

Acknowledgements
The publisher and authors would like to thank the following for permission to use photographs and other copyright material:

Cover: © Mohamad Itani/Trevillion Images

p7: Leemage/Getty Images; **p10:** Warner Bros/REX/Shutterstock; **p15:** © Ken Howard; **p18:** Eliot Elisofon/Getty Images; **p21:** Shutterstock; **p24:** John D. Kisch/Separate Cinema Archive/Getty Images; **p26:** SNAP/REX/Shutterstock; **pp32-36:** Alastair Muir/REX/Shutterstock; **p38:** CBS Photo Archive/Getty Images; **p40:** Moviestore Collection/REX/Shutterstock; **p42:** Warner Bros/REX/Shutterstock; **p46:** Robbie Jack - Corbis/Getty Images; **p53:** Alastair Muir/REX/Shutterstock; **p60:** Bettmann/Getty Images; **p62:** iStockphoto; **p64:** Shutterstock; **p68:** Warner Bros/REX/Shutterstock; **p70:** Alastair Muir/REX/Shutterstock; **p77:** Henry Bush/Associated Newspapers/REX/Shutterstock; **p79:** © Photostage; **p82:** Alexandra Davenport; **p86:** © Photostage.

We are grateful for permission to reprint the following copyright texts:

Extracts from Tennessee Williams: *A Streetcar Named Desire* (Penguin Classics, 2009), copyright © 1947, 1953 by The University of the South, reprinted by permission of Georges Borchardt, Inc, for the Estate of Tennessee Williams. All rights reserved.

Michael Billington: extract from Review of *A Streetcar Named Desire*, theguardian.com, 29 July 2009, copyright © Guardian News and Media 2016, reprinted by permission of GNM Ltd.

Robert Bray: extracts from '*A Streetcar Named Desire* - the political and historical subtext' in Philip C Kolin (Ed): *Confronting Tennessee Williams's A Streetcar Named Desire: Essays in Critical Pluralism* (Greenwood Press, 1993), reprinted by permission of ABC-Clio Inc via Copyright Clearance Center, Inc

Anton Chekhov: 'Uncle Vanya' in *Chekhov: Five Major Plays* translated by Ronald Hingley (Oxford Classics, 1977), reprinted by permission of Oxford University Press.

John M Clum: extracts from 'The sacrificial stud and the fugitive female in *Suddenly Last Summer*, *Orpheus Descending* and *Sweet Bird of Youth*', in Matthew C Roudané (Ed): *The Cambridge Companion to Tennessee Williams* (Cambridge, 1997), reprinted by permission of Cambridge University Press.

Lyn Gardner: 'My disability helped me understand Blanche DuBois, says *Streetcar* actor', theguardian.com, 2 June 2014, copyright © Guardian News and Media 2016, reprinted by permission of GNM Ltd.

Ronald Hayman: extracts from *Tennessee Willliams: Everyone Else is an Audience* (Yale University Press, 1993), copyright © Ronald Hayman 1993, reprinted by permission of Yale Representation Ltd.

Philip C Kolin: extract from 'Eunice Hubbel and the feminist thematics of *A Streetcar Named Desire*', in Philip C Kolin (Ed): *Confronting Tennessee Williams's A Streetcar Named Desire: Essays in Critical Pluralism* (Greenwood Press, 1993), reprinted by permission of ABC-Clio Inc via Copyright Clearance Center, Inc; extract from *Williams: A Streetcar Named Desire* (Cambridge, 2000), reprinted by permission of Cambridge University Press.

John Lahr: extract from *Tennessee Williams: Mad Pilgrimage of the Flesh* (Bloomsbury, 2015), copyright © John Lahr 2014, reprinted by permission of Bloomsbury Circus, an imprint of Bloomsbury Publishing Plc and of W W Norton and Company, Inc.

Felicia Hardison Londre: extracts from 'A streetcar running fifty years' in Matthew C Roudané (Ed): *The Cambridge Companion to Tennessee Williams* (Cambridge, 1997), reprinted by permission of Cambridge University Press.

Camille Paglia: extract from review of *A Streetcar Named Desire*, 3 December 1947, copyright © Camille Paglia 1947, published in *A New Literary History of America* edited by Greil Marcus and Werner Sollors (Harvard University Press, 2009), reprinted by permission of the author.

Adrian Poole: extracts from *Tragedy: A Very Short Introduction* (OUP, 2005), copyright © Adrian Poole 2005, reprined by permission of Oxford University Press.

Sophocles: 'Oedipus Rex', in *Sophocles: The Theban Plays* translated by E F Watling (Penguin, 1947, 1984), translation copyright © E F Watling 1947, reprinted by permission of Penguin Books Ltd.

Nancy Tischler: extract from 'Romantic textures in Williams' plays and short stories' in Matthew C Roudané (Ed): *The Cambridge Companion to Tennessee Williams* (Cambridge, 1997), reprinted by permission of Cambridge University Press.

Tennessee Williams: extract from an interview with Cecil Brown (1974) from *Conversations with Tennessee Williams* edited by A J Devlin (Univ of Mississippi, 1986), copyright © 1986 by The University Press of Mississippi, reprinted by permission of Georges Borchardt, Inc, for the Estate of Tennessee Williams. All rights reserved.

We have tried to trace and contact all copyright holders before publication. If notified, the publishers will be pleased to rectify any errors or omissions at the earliest opportunity.